The Czech Republic

Second Edition

STEVEN OTFINOSKI

®

Facts On File, Inc.

Nations in Transition: The Czech Republic, Second Edition

Facts On File, Inc.
132 West 31st Street
New York NY 10001

Library of Congress Cataloging-in-Publication Data

Otfinoski, Steven
    The Czech Republic / Steven Otfinoski.—2nd ed.
        p. cm. — (Nations in transition)
    Includes bibliographical references and index.
    ISBN 0-8160-5083-X
    1. Czech Republic. I. Title. II. Series.
    DB2011.O87 2004
    943.7105—dc22   2003063060

Text design by Erika K. Arroyo
Cover design by Nora Wertz
Maps by Pat Meschino © Facts On File, Inc.

Printed in the United States of America

MP FOF 10 9 8 7 6 5 4 3 2 1

This book is printed on acid-free paper.

CONTENTS

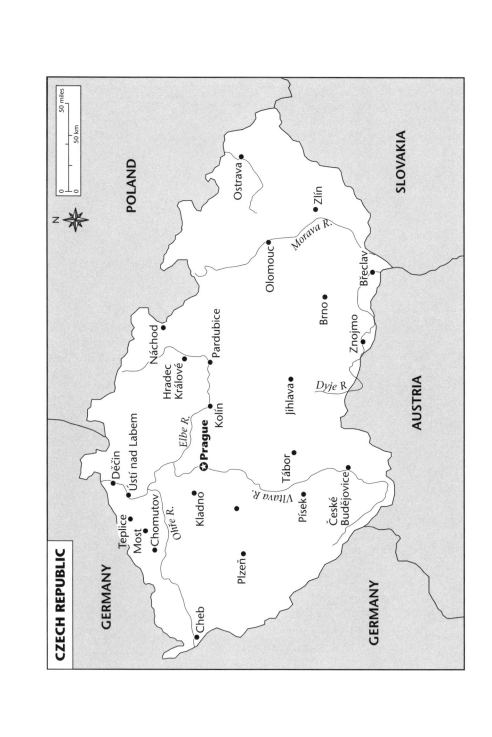

INTRODUCTION

In August 2002 the city of Prague, the Czech Republic's beloved capital city, was under siege. The attack, unlike those of the past, was not mounted by a human enemy but nature. A week of torrential rains caused the Vltava River to overflow its banks and bring about the worst flooding the small nation had seen in more than a century.

Two hundred thousand Czechs evacuated their homes for higher ground, 40,000 of them in the vicinity of Prague. Left behind were age-old buildings in Prague's venerable Old Town, many of them filled with priceless art treasures. This irreplaceable cultural heritage might have been lost in the rising flood tide if not for the efforts of a Moravian businessman, Ladislav Srubek, who financed the building of a fencelike structure on the banks of the Vltava consisting of interlocking aluminum slats. The sturdy barrier saved much of Old Town from the water's fury. While the nation suffered billions of dollars in damages, nearly all of Prague's historic sites were spared. Srubek was hailed as "the man who saved Prague" and his barrier referred to as "the Wall of Hope."

Just as nature threatened to sweep away centuries of a rich cultural heritage, so today equally powerful forces are threatening the economy and social well-being of this proud country. The stability and prosperity that made the Czech Republic the envy of its neighbors in eastern Europe in the first decade of freedom after communism's downfall were shattered by a political and economic crisis in 1997. Since then this nation of 10 million has been struggling to regain its footing. At times there seems to be no Wall of Hope to hold back the rising tides of confusion, turmoil, and cynicism, but the Czechs, known for their common sense, practicality, and inventiveness, trudge on. They know that in the final analysis they will not only survive but prevail.

At the Crossroads of Europe

The Czech Republic, established January 1, 1993, is one of the newest nations in eastern Europe. However, the land and its statehood are centuries old. In a part of Europe that has seen change and strife throughout its long history, the Czechs have endured their share of upheaval.

When talking about the Czech land, *lands* is the more appropriate word. Three distinct regions developed here in the center of Europe, sharing a common language, culture, and ethnic background: Bohemia, Moravia, and Silesia.

An independent part of the Holy Roman Empire, the Czech lands were later subjugated by the Austrian Empire for three centuries. Then in 1918, following World War I, the Czechs and their neighbors, the Slovaks, joined to form a new and independent nation called Czechoslovakia. It was to become one of the most democratic nations in eastern Europe during the next 20 years. Czechoslovakia survived both the Nazi occupation of World War II and the more than 40-year reign of the Communists following that war, but it could not survive either freedom in 1990 or internal turmoil between the Czechs and Slovaks—two peoples closely joined by blood but separated by their political and economic past.

Throughout all these changes, the Czechs have retained their ingenuity, their industry, and their imagination. Inhabitants of one of the most highly industrialized nations in eastern Europe, with a standard of living that is the envy of its neighbors, the Czechs have always balanced materialism with intellectual concerns. Their national heroes are innovators and rugged individualists—Jan Hus, the rebel priest who defied the pope and prefigured the Protestant Reformation by more than a century; Franz Kafka, the quiet Jewish writer whose bizarre, metaphorical stories and novels ushered in the psychological literature expressive of the 20th century's anxiety and alienation; Alexander Dubček, the courageous Communist leader who for a brief time gave socialism "a human face"; and Václav Havel, the playwright who became his country's number-one dissenter against the Communists and the new republic's first head of state. Where else but in the Czech Republic could a playwright become president of his country?

The Czech people are individualists, as American writer Patricia Hampl discovered while riding a streetcar in Prague:

> The tram was crowded, as trams in Prague usually are. I had to stand at the back, wedged in with a lot of other people. . . . Then I saw, very near to me, the falconer and his bird. A man, dressed in green like a true man of the forest in knee pants with high leather boots and a green leather short jacket. On his head he wore a cap of soft velvet, possibly suede, with a feather on the side. But most incredible was the falcon that clove to his gloved hand with its lacquered claws, its head covered with a tiny leather mask topped, as the hunter's own cap was, with a small, stiff plume. . . . The falconer seemed perfectly at ease in the back of the crowded car, when he got off, at the Slavia stop, next to the National Theater, and stood waiting for a connecting tram, it was the rest of the world and not he that looked inappropriate. . . . They struck me as emblems of the nation.

The Land and People

The Czech Republic is one of the smallest countries in eastern Europe, consisting of 30,449 square miles (78,864 sq km). Poland, one of its nearest neighbors, is four times the size of the Czech Republic. Only Slovakia and Albania are smaller. The country's population is 10,287,100 (2004 estimate). About 94 percent of the people are ethnic Czechs, and about 3 percent are Slovak. The remaining fraction of the population is made up of Hungarians, Poles, Germans, Ukrainians, and Romanies (Gypsies). Nearly three-quarters of the people live in urban areas.

Completely landlocked, the Czech Republic is bordered on the north by Poland and Germany, on the south by Austria, on the southeast and east by Slovakia, and on the northwest and west by Germany. In the center of central Europe, the Czech lands have often been called the "crossroads of Europe," which helps explain their importance historically as a place where both goods and ideas are exchanged.

Hradčany Castle, also known as Prague Castle, looms over the Czech Republic's capital city. The Vltava River flows in the foreground. (Courtesy Free Library of Philadelphia)

Bohemia

Geographically the Czech Republic is divided into three regions— Bohemia, Moravia, and Silesia—each with its own past and traditions. Bohemia is the largest and westernmost part of the country. It is basically a flat plateau surrounded by mountains and forests. The Bohemian Mountains, which are comprised of the Ore Mountains on the northwest German border and the Bohemian Forest to the southwest, are actually large hills rising about 2,500 feet (762 m) above sea level. The Ore Mountains are rich in coal and uranium ore, while the Bohemian Forest produces lumber and other wood products. Fertile soil covers the mountains, making them perfect for raising crops and livestock. They also draw thousands of Czechs and foreign tourists each year to their ski resorts and health spas.

To the northeast lie the Sudetic Mountains, which border Poland and are more rugged and higher than the Bohemian Mountains. The highest peak in the Czech Republic, Sněžka (5,256 feet, 1,602.5 m), is found here. The mountains are home to a number of important industrial cities and towns. The Bohemian-Moravian Highlands are on the west and extend through a good part of southern Bohemia into southwestern Moravia. Most of the region is farmland, although Plzeň (pronounced Pilsen), its largest city, is well known for its many breweries. The Bohemian Basin, the heart of the region, has farmland that is irrigated by the country's two major rivers—the Vltava (Moldau), flowing northward and the Elbe, flowing westward. Prague, the country's capital and largest city, lies along the Vltava in north-central Bohemia.

For centuries Czech poets, composers, and artists have praised the natural beauty of the Bohemian rivers and woodlands, perhaps none more eloquently than composer Bedřich Smetana (1824–84), the father of Czech classical music. In "The Moldau," one part of his six-movement epic symphonic poem *Má vlast (My Fatherland)* (1874–79), Smetana re-created the river's progress in sound. Here is an excerpt from the written preface to the score:

> Two springs pour forth their streams in the shade of the Bohemian forest, the one warm and gushing, the other cold and tranquil. Their waves, joyfully flowing over their rocky beds, unite and sparkle in the morning sun. The first brook, rushing on, becomes the River Moldau, which with its waters speeding through Bohemia's valleys, grows into a mighty stream. . . . At the Rapids of St. John the stream speeds on, winding its way through cataracts and hewing the path for its foaming waters through the rocky chasm into the broad river-bed in which it flows on in majestic calm toward Prague. . . .

Moravia

To the east of Bohemia is Moravia, a region of lowlands that is home to industry and mining. Brno, in the southwest, is the country's second largest city and one of Europe's largest textile centers. While Bohemia is larger and more historically celebrated, Moravians have their own regional pride, as writer Hampl learned during a brief stopover in Brno:

> Moravia is distinguished from Bohemia by a more elusive cultural quality. Moravians think of themselves as the *real* Czechs. Joseph Wechsberg,

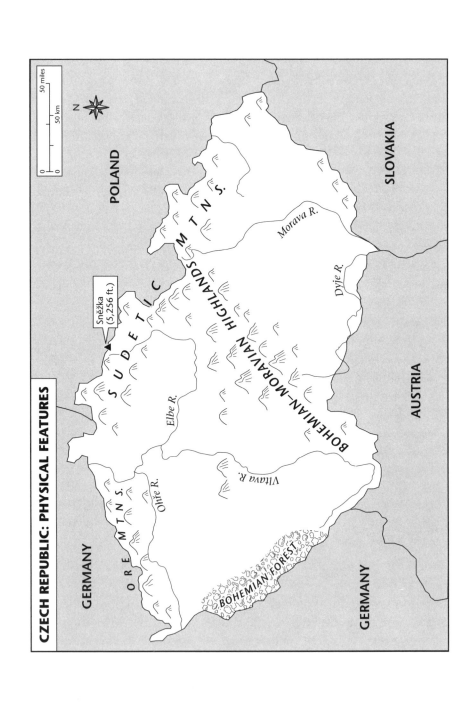

CZECH REPUBLIC: PHYSICAL FEATURES

GERMANY

POLAND

SLOVAKIA

AUSTRIA

GERMANY

O R E   M T N S.

S U D E T I C   M T N S.

BOHEMIAN-MORAVIAN HIGHLANDS

BOHEMIAN FOREST

Sněžka
(5,256 ft.)

Ohře R.

Elbe R.

Vltava R.

Morava R.

Dyje R.

N

50 miles
50 km

a Moravian himself, says the attitude of Moravians toward the rest of the Czechs is rather like that of a Boston Yankee to the West. . . . As we passed by a scaffolded old building, she [a Czech friend] pointed and said, "Older than Prague."

The Morava River, the easternmost part of Moravia, forms a fertile valley where many crops are grown. Still further to the northeast is Ostrava, an industrial center where coal is mined and iron and steel are produced.

Silesia

The third historical region, tiny Silesia, straddles the Czech Republic and Poland. Czech Silesia, the smaller of the two sections, contains the Karviná Basin, a rich source of coal. The black smoke that rises from its coal-fueled factories has given it the name the Black Country. The northern section of Silesia is characterized by wooded but fertile lowland used for farming vegetables.

Climate

The climate of the Czech Republic is somewhere between maritime and continental, with mildly cold winters and warm summers. Average temperatures range from 29°F (-2°C) in January to 66°F (19°C) in July. The average annual precipitation is 28 inches (71 cm).

The Czech Republic is a lovely land of rolling hills, pleasant farms, and historic but bustling cities. The Czechs are justifiably proud of their well-crafted goods, their fine crops, and their world-famous beer. They are also proud of the restless, creative minds that have produced model nation-states and great works of literature, music, and cinema. The often-troubled history of this practical people with a rich imagination has put both these sides of their national character to the supreme test.

NOTES
p. v "'The man who saved Prague'" and "'the Wall of Hope'" *New York Times*, August 18, 2002, p. 6.

p. vii   "'The tram was crowded . . .'" Patricia Hampl, A *Romantic Education* (Boston: Houghton Mifflin, 1981), pp. 208–209.

p. ix   "'Two springs pour forth . . .'" Liner notes, recording of Bedřich Smetana's "The Moldau," My *Fatherland,* performed by the Cleveland Orchestra, CBS's Great Performances series.

pp. ix–xi   "'Moravia is distinguished from Bohemia . . .'" Hampl, A *Romantic Education, p.* 257.

PART I
History

1

FROM MEDIEVAL KINGDOM TO MODERN NATION-STATE (PREHISTORY TO 1918)

More than 2,500 years ago the Czech people lived on the plains of central Asia and what is now Russia with their fellow Slavs, the Slovaks. They were a hard-working and peaceful people, preferring farming and raising livestock to warfare. This made them an attractive target for a barbaric tribe from the East, the Avars. These Mongolian invaders drove the Czechs and Slovaks westward in about A.D. 500, enslaving them in the region of central Europe that they inhabit to this day.

Under the strong leadership of their tribal chief Samo, the Slavs rose up against the Avars in 620 and defeated them. Determined to keep their freedom, the Czechs and Slovaks built permanent settlements of wood and stone with strong defense points. About a century later two Greek missionaries, Saints Cyril (ca. 827–869) and Methodius (ca. 825–884), arrived in the Czech lands and brought Christianity to these pagan people. They also taught them a new alphabet, later known as Cyrillic, after Cyril, who developed it from the Greek alphabet.

By 800 the Czechs and Slovaks had joined other Slavic tribes to form the Great Moravian Empire, which encompassed much of central Europe.

But the empire was short lived. The Magyars, fierce warriors from neighboring Hungary, invaded their land and destroyed the empire. They took over Slovakia, making the Slovaks their vassals for the next thousand years. The more-fortunate Czechs, however, escaped Hungarian domination and went on to found their own kingdom.

The Rise of Bohemia

About 800 Queen Libussa and her consort, the peasant Přemysl, founded the first Czech royal dynasty. The Romans, who had invaded the area centuries earlier, had named it Boiohaemia, after a Celtic tribe, the Boii, who were driven out by the Czechs when they first entered the region. For the next four centuries the Premysl kings ruled over the kingdom of Bohemia.

The first great historical Bohemian ruler was Wenceslas (ca. 907–929), a Bohemian prince whose piety is celebrated in the still-popular Christmas carol that bears his name. Wenceslas worked hard to establish Christianity in Bohemia and forged an alliance with his former enemy, Henry I of Germany. Under Wenceslas,

"Good King Wenceslas" was too good for this world and was murdered by his brother. This 15th-century portrait of Bohemia's patron saint hangs in the Church of St. Nicholas in Prague. (Courtesy Free Library of Philadelphia)

Bohemia and Moravia were united under a single crown, but his allegiance to Christianity earned him the hatred of the nobility, who were supported by Wenceslas's brother, Boleslav the Cruel (d. 967). In 929 Boleslav assassinated Wenceslas as the latter was going to church; he then seized the throne—his major aim—and further promoted Christianity. By the next century Wenceslas (Václav in Czech) was recognized as the patron saint of Bohemia.

KING CHARLES IV (1316–1378)

If any one person was responsible for the Golden Age of Bohemia, it was Charles IV, king of Germany and Bohemia and eventually Holy Roman Emperor.

He was born in Prague, the city he would one day make great, the eldest son of John of Luxembourg, king of Bohemia. At age eight, as was the custom among royalty, Charles was married to Blanche, sister of Philip IV of France. His close friendship with Pope Clement VI, who helped him become king of Germany in 1346, earned him the nickname "the priests' king."

When his father died a month later defending France from the English at the Battle of Crécy, Charles became king of Bohemia. In 1354 he crossed the Alps to reach Rome, where he was crowned Holy Roman Emperor. Prague was now the capital of the empire, and Charles saw that the city looked the part. He rebuilt the Cathedral of St. Vitus in the lighter, more luminous French style, constructed castles that seemed to soar, laid out the neat streets of Prague's New Town, and founded Charles University in 1348, the oldest university in central Europe.

Charles was an enthusiastic patron of the arts and entertained the Italian poet Petrarch and other writers and intellectuals in Prague. Fluent in five languages, he helped the development of the written German language. His Golden Bull, a decree issued in 1356, made the state secure from papal interference by entrusting the selection of future emperors to seven electors. It also assured the kingdom of Bohemia the right of self-government within the empire. This bull would remain in force until the downfall of the Holy Roman Empire in 1806.

A strong and wise monarch, Charles secured the succession for his eldest son, Wenceslas, before his death. He was buried in St. Vitus, one of the many monuments that he left the people of Prague.

A statue of Charles IV stands in Prague. One of the greatest kings of Bohemia, he ushered in its golden age in the 14th century. (Courtesy Library of Congress)

Boleslav soon found himself at the mercy of the German king Otto I, who incorporated Bohemia into his Holy Roman Empire (a Christian state centered in Germany that claimed to continue the tradition of the fallen Roman Empire). Although a part of the empire, Bohemia largely retained its right to self-government.

The next great Bohemian king was Charles IV (see boxed biography), who succeeded his father, the blind but valiant King John (1296–1346), killed at the Battle of Crécy in France, while fighting against the English. Charles quickly proved an outstanding state builder. In his 30-year reign he made Bohemia one of the greatest kingdoms in medieval Europe. Many of the fine churches and other structures Charles had built, such as the Cathedral of St. Vitus and Charles Bridge, the only bridge to span the Vltava River until the 19th century, still stand today. His greatest achievement was Charles University in Prague, founded in 1348, the first institution of higher learning in central Europe. In 1355 Charles was crowned Holy Roman Emperor and made Prague the capital of his empire.

Religious Reform and the Hussite Movement

But the Golden Age of Bohemia would be quickly followed by a time of darkness and division. As one historian has wryly observed, the Holy Roman Empire was not holy, was not Roman, and was not an empire. The Roman Catholic Church shared the power of the state with royalty, and high church officials abused their privilege at the people's expense. In Prague, a priest, Jan Hus (see boxed biography), dared to speak out against the corruption of the church and called for a movement back to the simple teachings of Christ as set down in the Bible. The fact that Hus preached to the people not in German, the established language of the church and state, but in his native Czech, made him an even greater threat to the upper classes: Hus's religious rebellion was also a social and nationalistic one. As rector of the University of Prague, Hus gathered a faithful following in the city and surrounding areas until he was excommunicated by the pope for his outspokenness in 1411. The Germans tricked him into coming to the Council of Constance in Germany in 1414 to explain his actions. Once there, he was arrested, tried, and condemned as a heretic. In July 1415 Hus was burned at the stake for defying the power of the church.

Hus's death made him a martyr to his followers, called Hussites. For the next two decades the Hussites, anti-Catholic Bohemian nationalists, fought against the Catholic Holy Roman Empire in the Hussite Wars. The conflict finally ended in 1436 in compromise, allowing the Hussites some freedom of worship, but by then many of them had fled Bohemia and were living as wandering exiles in Europe. They gave a new meaning to the word *Bohemian*, which is still used to describe a person who lives an unconventional lifestyle. Many of these Bohemians later settled in the United States, where they found the religious freedom they had been searching for. Unfortunately the corruption they had fought against continued to grow and infect every part of the Bohemian state.

Czech nobles, anxious to retain their own power, brought in foreign kings from Poland whom they could control. Weak and divided, Bohemia

---

JAN HUS (1372–1415)

The Protestant Reformation of the 16th century was anticipated more than 100 years earlier by this greatest of Czech religious reformers. Jan Hus was born in southwest Bohemia in the village of Husince. He was known as "Jan of Husince" and later dropped all but the first three letters of the village's name. Although a peasant by birth, Hus had a brilliant mind and was accepted into the University of Prague in 1390. Ten years later he was ordained a priest in the Roman Catholic Church and made dean of the faculty the following year.

The clergy in Bohemia, who owned about half of all the land in the country, frequently abused their power. Hus, under the influence of the great English reformer John Wycliffe (ca. 1330–84), attacked the church leaders, calling the papacy an "institution of Satan." A strong nationalist, Hus preached publicly in Czech at a time when most clerics spoke in the dominant German language.

Although accused by church leaders of heresy, Hus had powerful protectors in the archbishop of Prague and King Wenceslas IV of Bohemia. In 1409 he was appointed rector of the university but was excommunicated in 1412 by the church for his fiery preaching against clerical abuse.

In 1414 King Sigismund of Germany, Wenceslas's half brother, persuaded Hus to come to Germany to argue his case in Constance. Hus agreed but soon found he had been tricked into leaving the safety of Prague. He was arrested upon his arrival and put in prison. During three public hearings Hus defended himself convincingly. Given the chance to recant his teachings, he refused and was sentenced to death. He was

finally fell prey to neighboring Austria, ruled, as the Holy Roman Empire was, by one of Europe's most powerful dynasties, the Hapsburgs.

Revolt and Defeat

In 1526 Hapsburg emperor Ferdinand I (1503–64) became ruler over Bohemia, although the kingdom retained some of its independence. About the same time the Protestant Reformation, led by Martin Luther in Germany, swept across Europe. Many Czechs, longing to be freed from

burned at the stake, the common sentence for heretics, on July 6, 1415. Made a national hero by his death, Hus was later declared a martyr to his faith by the University of Prague. His reforms lived on in his followers, who called themselves Hussites and later divided into two groups, conservatives and radicals. The conservatives made a peaceful treaty with the Catholic Church in 1433 and were granted the right to worship. The radicals fought the church and were defeated the following year. In 1457 some Hussites formed the Unity of Brethren, based on Hus's teachings, and later became the Moravian Church. The Moravian Church still flourishes today in the Czech Republic, other European countries, and the United States.

Religious reformer Jan Hus defends himself at his trial in Constance, Germany. Although he ably defended himself, Hus was condemned as a heretic and burned at the stake. (Courtesy Free Library of Philadelphia)

the Catholic Hapsburgs, became Protestants. The emperor sent in priests belonging to the Society of Jesus (Jesuits), a scholarly religious order founded in 1534 by Saint Ignatius Loyola, to restore Catholicism to heretic Bohemia. When Ferdinand's descendant, Emperor Matthias, refused to grant them religious freedom, members of the Bohemian parliament threw two of his councilors out the window of Prague's Hradčany Castle in May 1618. This was an old Bohemian punishment for unjust or corrupt officials.

The incident sparked The Thirty Years' War, a religious conflict between Protestants and Roman Catholics. From Bohemia the war spread to Protestant Denmark and Sweden, who opposed the Catholic German states. In its last phase the war became a purely political struggle between the Bourbon dynasty of France and the Hapsburgs, who ruled Germany and Austria. The army of Emperor Matthias decisively defeated the Czech nobles at the Battle of the White Mountain in 1620. The proud kingdom of Bohemia was reduced to a fiefdom of the Hapsburgs. The kingdom was divided into three parts—Bohemia, Moravia, and Silesia. The cultural heritage of the Czechs was wiped out as the zealous Jesuits burned whole libraries of precious books containing the glory of Czech literature. The Czechs were forced to give up their language and to speak and write in German. Roman Catholicism became the state religion, and Czech culture and traditions were cruelly suppressed. The Hapsburgs, however, could not wrench the idea of their nation from the hearts of the people.

The 19th-Century Nationalist Movement

Their national identity ruthlessly repressed, the Czechs found other channels for their energies. The Industrial Revolution that swept England in the late 18th century erupted in Bohemia and Moravia. While their neighbors in eastern Europe were still living in a basically agricultural society as they had for centuries, the Czechs were developing factories and other industrial works at an incredible rate. Peasants from the countryside swarmed into the cities to work in these new factories and businesses. Cities such as Prague and Brno developed into centers of intellectualism as well as industry; out of this intellectual ferment arose a new spirit of Slavic pride and Czech nationalism. The leading light of this

Pan-Slavic movement was writer and historian František Palacký (1798–1876). In his monumental *History of the Czech Nation* (1836–67), Palacký viewed the history of his people as an ongoing struggle between the Slavs and the Germans that would end in the reemergence of the Czech lands as a free and independent republic. He did not advocate a violent revolution to accomplish this, but he fostered self-affirmation through education.

Although nonviolent, Palacký was steadfast in his nationalism. When invited in 1848 by the German congress in Frankfurt to hold elections in his homeland for representatives to a constitutional convention meant to establish a new federation of German states, he wrote back

> I am not a German. . . . I am a Czech of Slavonic blood. . . . That nation is a small one, it is true, but from time immemorial it has been a nation by itself and depends upon its own strength. Its rulers were from ancient times members of the federation of German princes, but the nation never regarded itself as belonging to the German nation, nor throughout all these centuries has it been regarded by others as so belonging. . . . I must briefly express my conviction that those who ask that Austria and with her Bohemia should unite on national lines with Germany, are demanding that she should commit suicide—a step lacking either moral or political sense. . . .

Palacký died in 1876, never seeing his dream of a Czech republic fulfilled. However, he inspired young men such as Tomáš Masaryk (see boxed biography, Chapter 2) and Edvard Beneš (1884–1948), both of whom would help transform that dream into reality.

In 1867 the Hapsburgs' Austrian Empire joined with Hungary to form the Austro-Hungarian Empire. After a thousand years of separation fate had joined the Czechs and Slovaks once again. This time they would suffer jointly as subjects of the same tyrannical master. Increased taxation and economic misery turned the national movement more radical, with more and more Czech reformers calling for complete separation from the Austrians and the Hungarians as the only solution.

In 1914 World War I broke out. The Austro-Hungarian Empire sided with the Germans against England, France, and (after 1917) the United States. Czechs and Slovaks were drafted to fight, but many deserted rather than help their despised masters win the war. As the conflict wore on, revolutionary ferment increased in the Czech lands. Many national- ist leaders were arrested, but Masaryk and Beneš escaped and fled to France. In Paris in 1916 they helped found the Czechoslovak national council, an organization dedicated to gaining support from the Allies for an independent, democratic state for their peoples.

The war ended in German defeat and the complete dismantling of the Austro-Hungarian Empire; freedom was granted to Bohemia, Moravia, and Silesia. But Masaryk knew that to survive in a new Europe, the old Slavic tribes of Czechs and Slovaks would have to join together. So in 1919, at the Treaty of Versailles, with the full support of the United States and its allies, a new nation was born—the republic of Czechoslovakia.

NOTE
p. 11 "'I am not a German. . . .'" S. Harrison Thomson, *Czechoslovakia in European History* (Princeton, N.J.: Princeton University Press, 1943), pp. 45–46.

2

Czechoslovakia under Two Brutal Masters (1918–1985)

The new nation of Czechoslovakia was only one of a number of new and independent countries to rise out of the ashes of World War I—the others included Poland, Hungary, and Yugoslavia—but none got off to a more promising start. Tomáš Masaryk was elected the country's first president, and he worked effectively to make Czechoslovakia a model of capitalist democracy. A new constitution was drawn up and implemented, and industry grew and expanded.

But there were serious problems to be faced. The economy was in flux, unemployment was rampant, and ethnic unrest was on the rise. The Czechs made up only 51 percent of the population, but they controlled the government. The Slovaks, poorer and less urbanized than the Czechs, were justifiably upset. To worsen the situation, 3.5 million Germans living in the Sudetic Mountains area known as Sudetenland were clamoring for their own rights. For all his good intentions Masaryk did little to alleviate the ethnic unrest, and by the 1930s the division between the Czechs and the rest of the populace was a serious one.

In 1935, after 16 years in power, Masaryk resigned as president. His longtime colleague Edvard Beneš succeeded him. Beneš did his best to continue Masaryk's policies, but Europe had become a more troubled place

Edvard Beneš (center), second president of a democratic Czechoslovakia, is at work with Foreign Minister Nicolas Titulesco (left) of Romania and Foreign Minister Bevgoljub Jevtic of Yugoslavia. He remained in office only for three years before the Germans invaded and seized control of his country. (Courtesy Free Library of Philadelphia)

than it had been in 1918. In Germany, Adolf Hitler (1889–1945) had come to power and promised to restore Germany to its former glory before the humiliating defeat of World War I. Part of that glory rested on conquering new lands and subjecting their peoples to German imperialism.

The Nazi Occupation and World War II

In March 1938 Hitler's troops marched into Austria, his nation's former ally, and were greeted in the streets as liberators. Next, Hitler turned his attention to the Sudetenland of Czechoslovakia. Hitler warned the Czechs that unless they granted self-rule to the Sudeten Germans, he would declare war. In September 1938 Prime Minister Neville Chamberlain (1869–1940) of Great Britain and French premier Édouard Daladier (1884–1970) met in Munich, Germany, with Hitler and his ally, Benito Mussolini (1883–1945), Italy's Fascist leader. The Czechs were not invited to attend. Hitler assured the other leaders that he would make no further territorial claims in Europe if they allowed him to take the Sudetenland. Chamberlain and Daladier, anxious to avoid war, agreed not to interfere, although both had previously supported Czechoslovakia. Chamberlain returned to Great Britain from the Munich Pact proclaiming he had helped make "peace for our time."

But in Czechoslovakia the time for peace had ended. Unable to resist Hitler's Nazi troops, the Czechs reluctantly seceded the Sudetenland to him in 1938. With this occurrence President Beneš and the legitimate democratic government fled the country and set up a government-in-exile in London.

In early 1939 Hitler's troops marched into Prague and made the entire country a German "protectorate." None of Czechoslovakia's allies came to its defense. When Hitler invaded Poland a few months later, western Europe realized, too late, that the German dictator was bent on dominating all of Europe. Two days later England and France declared war on Germany, and World War II was under way.

A mostly German crowd in Sudetenland salutes German dictator Adolf Hitler for "liberating" them from Czechoslovakia in 1938. Hitler would use the Sudetenland issue as an excuse to occupy all of Czechoslovakia. (Courtesy Library of Congress)

The Soviet Union, a Communist dictatorship, offered to help Czechoslovakia if the western allies followed suit; the democratic Czech government-in-exile gave full support to the western powers and the Soviet Union. The Czech and Slovak Communist Party therefore helped the war resistance within the country during the long German occupation. These two actions made the Czechs look more sympathetically on the Communists than on the western powers.

One of the first countries to come under Nazi control in the war, Czechoslovakia escaped the wholesale destruction that befell many of its neighbors in eastern Europe, but the Czechs did not survive the war unscathed. When the Nazi governor of Prague, Reinhard Heydrich, was assassinated in 1942, the Nazis exacted a brutal revenge: The entire adult male populations of the Czech towns of Lidice and Ležáky were executed, the women were sent to concentration camps, and the children sent to their deaths in mobile gas chambers.

František Kraus, a concentration-camp survivor, was part of a work gang assigned to dig mass graves at Lidice during the slaughter. Here is how he remembers the grim event in his essay included in the anthology *Art from the Ashes:*

> The air rages like a wounded cyclop and hurtles the deadly rocks down to us again. Bricks drop onto the empty church benches, jump high again and dance to and fro as if it were a festive church holiday, then the beams clatter down and break the roof, walls and vaultings shake, pictures of saints in gold frames fall from the old walls, and thunder to the ground.

When the Slovak Communist Party staged an uprising in August 1944, it was ruthlessly put down by the Nazis. But the Germans had taken on too many enemies and ultimately lost the war. In early 1945 Czechoslovakia was liberated by Soviet troops from the east and U.S. troops from the west. By the war's end, 360,000 Czechs and Slovaks had died.

The Communists Take Over

Beneš returned to set up a new government, but he found himself taking on a new unwelcome partner in power—the Communists. Many Czechs,

A professor of philosophy and sociology at Charles University, Tomáš Masaryk used his ideas and theories on government to transform Czechoslovakia into a model democracy in the two decades between the world wars. This photograph was taken by noted Czech author Karel Čapek. (Courtesy Library of Congress)

however, were grateful to the Communists, who had stood by them in resisting the Nazis. They praised the Communist plan to appropriate land from the 3 million deported Sudeten Germans and redistribute it to Czech and Slovak peasants.

In the election of 1946 the Communist Party won 38 percent of the vote. Beneš, reelected president, formed a new coalition government— the National Front—with the Communists. Communist Party leader Klement Gottwald (1896–1953) was named premier. About half of the government ministers were Communists and half noncommunist. One of the most influential of the noncommunist leaders was Foreign Minister Jan Masaryk (1886–1948), son of the late president.

In 1947 Masaryk met personally with Joseph Stalin (1879–1953), dictator of the Soviet Union, who urged him not to accept U.S. aid through the Marshall Plan but to rely on Russia's help. "I went to Moscow as the foreign minister of a sovereign state and I came back a stooge of Stalin," Masaryk later said. When the 11 noncommunist government ministers resigned en masse to protest Soviet influence in their affairs, the Communists simply filled their positions with party members. Fearing the worst was to come, many Czechs began to flee the country. Jan Masaryk, it was rumored, would soon be joining them.

On March 10, 1948, at 6:25 A.M., Masaryk's pajama-clad body was found in the courtyard of his apartment building. It was alleged that he had committed suicide by leaping to his death from his bathroom window, but many Czechs believed that he had been pushed from the window by thugs hired by the Communists to prevent his leaving the country and denouncing them. How Masaryk really died may never be known; in 1969 the Czech Communist government retracted the suicide story and tried to convince the world that the former foreign minister fell

TOMÁŠ MASARYK (1850–1937)

Václav Havel, first president of the postcommunist Czech Republic, was not the first writer-thinker to be the leader of his people. He was preceded by Czechoslovakia's founder and first president, Tomáš Masaryk. An author and philosophy professor, Masaryk's thoughts on democracy and freedom helped make his homeland Europe's model democracy during his long presidency.

Masaryk was born in Moravia, and his father was the coachman to the Austrian emperor Francis Joseph. He studied at the Universities of Vienna and Leipzig and married an American, Charlotte Garrigue. In 1882 Masaryk became professor of philosophy at the new Czech University of Prague, where he began a distinguished career as a teacher, thinker, and author.

A member of the Austro-Hungarian parliament from 1891, Masaryk became an outspoken supporter of the rights of the Czechs and Slovaks. Nine years later he launched the Czech Peoples Party, which called for the unity of the Czechs and Slovaks and national recognition from the Hapsburgs. When World War I broke out, he fled to Switzerland and then England. The Austro-Hungarian government sentenced Masaryk in absentia to death for high treason. Reaching America, he promoted independence for his country to President Woodrow Wilson.

At the war's end Masaryk helped found Czechoslovakia out of the ruins of the Austro-Hungarian Empire and became its president. For 17 years his wise and judicious leadership kept his nation in peace and prosperity, although the Slovaks were increasingly unhappy with his failure to recognize their rights more fully. In failing health, Masaryk resigned from office in 1935 and died two years later, mercifully spared the sight of his beloved country becoming a satellite, first to Nazi Germany and then to the Soviet Union.

to his death accidentally from a windowsill while "sitting in a yoga position to combat insomnia."

With most of the leaders of the opposition gone, the Czech Communists went to work recruiting people into their party. By the end of 1948 party membership had reached 2.5 million, or 18 percent of the population. No other country in Eastern Europe outside of the Soviet Union had such a high party membership. The Communists rewrote the Czech constitution to suit their own ends; rather than sign it, President Beneš resigned. A broken man, he died three months later.

Farms were collectivized and industry taken over by the Communist state. Private property no longer existed. The People's Democracy of Czechoslovakia was a democracy in name only. Personal freedom ended; the country became a police state.

Meanwhile, in nearby Yugoslavia in 1948, Communist leader Marshal Tito (1892–1980), who was born Josip Broz, did the unthinkable: He severed all relations with Stalin. The Soviet dictator fumed and grumbled, but Tito was too popular with the people of Yugoslavia to be uprooted and replaced by a Soviet puppet. Fearing that other Communist satellite countries might attempt to follow Tito's lead, Stalin decided that the time was right for a crackdown. Ironically, Czechoslovakia, where Stalin should have felt the most secure, received the brunt of his terror. Rudolf Slánský (1901–52), a loyal Stalinist who had arrested hundreds of Czechs in his leader's name, was charged in 1951 with conspiracy with the Jews to overthrow the republic and arrested with 12 other government officials. The resulting "show trials" were a carbon copy of the infamous Moscow trials of the 1930s where Stalin purged the party and the Soviet Union of so-called enemies.

Forced to make ridiculous public confessions of their "crimes," Slánský and 10 of his codefendants were found guilty in 1952 and condemned to death. Even in death they received no dignity from Stalin's executioners, as this excerpt from an article that appeared in a liberal Prague periodical in 1968 makes clear:

> When the eleven condemned had been executed, Referent D. [person being interviewed] found himself, by chance, at the Ruzyn with the [Soviet] adviser Golkin. Present at the meeting were the driver and the two referents who had been charged with the disposal of the

ashes. They announced they had placed them inside a potato sack and that they left for the vicinity of Prague with the intention of spreading the ashes in the fields. Noticing the ice-covered pavement, they laughed as he told that it had never before happened to him to be transporting fourteen persons at the same time in his Tatra [kind of automobile], the three living and the eleven contained in the sack.

In all, 180 politicians were executed in the purge trials, and an estimated 130,000 ordinary Czechs were arrested, imprisoned, and sent to labor camps or executed between 1948 and 1953.

Then in March 1953 Joseph Stalin died of a cerebral hemorrhage. The terror subsided as Stalin's lieutenants struggled for power. Nikita Khrushchev (1894–1971), the man who emerged as the new leader of the Soviet Union, denounced Stalin for some of his crimes against humanity in a "secret speech" delivered in 1956. The process of de-Stalinization— the end of Stalin hero-worship and subsequent liberalization of communism—had less effect in Czechoslovakia than in Hungary, Poland, and other Communist countries. Unfortunately the people who had done Stalin's bidding were still in power in Czechoslovakia.

What little light penetrated Czechoslovakia's Iron Curtain was shut out when Antonín Novotný (1904–75), general secretary of the Czech Communist Party, became president, replacing Antonín Zápotocký (1884–1957), who had died. Novotný was a hard-line Stalinist who toed the party line and quickly alienated his own people. By concentrating on the heavy industry the Soviets required and ignoring consumer products, Novotný helped created a serious recession in the early 1960s. Political unrest, spurred on by students and intellectuals, forced Novotný to make concessions and even get rid of other hard-liners in his government.

But the demonstrations continued. By late 1967 it was clear to Leonid Brezhnev (1906–82), Khrushchev's successor in the Kremlin, that Novotný could not control his people and would have to go. In January 1968 he was replaced as party general secretary by a mild-mannered 46-year-old Slovak, Alexander Dubček (see boxed biography). Little was known about Dubček other than he was a devoted, life-long Communist and had a personal integrity that most of his corrupt colleagues lacked.

The Prague Spring and Its Bitter Aftermath

In a few short weeks it was apparent that Dubček would be a very different kind of Communist leader than the men who had preceded him. In a speech before a group of Czech farmers he urged them to take the initiate to improve their lives and then opened the floor to hear their complaints and suggestions. When they spoke against party policy, Dubček listened. This open forum was repeated throughout the country in the weeks and months ahead. Dubček soon ended censorship: Writers, editors, and publishers were free to print the truth about the past, investigate the problems of the present, and lay down new plans for the future. The government approved experiments in a mixed economy that allowed for

A crowd of Czechoslovaks shake hands with national leader Alexander Dubček only a few weeks after a Soviet invasion had brought to an end his liberal reforms. (AP Photo)

ALEXANDER DUBČEK (1921–1992)

"It's been a hard life, but you cannot suppress an idea," said Alexander Dubček when, after 20 years in exile, his life's work was finally vindicated. Dubček's idea of a socialism that met the needs of his country's people challenged the authority of his Soviet masters for one shining moment, as no Eastern European government had before.

Dubček was not a likely person to reform the communist system: he'd been born in the small Slovakian town of Uhrover to a father who was a cabinet-maker and a founding member of the Czech Communist Party in 1925. The family lived in the Soviet Union for more than a decade, returning in 1938 just before the Nazi invasion. Young Dubček joined the Communist Party the following year, although it had been outlawed by the Nazis. He worked in the anti-Nazi underground and fought in the Slovak national uprising in 1944. During the fighting he was wounded twice, and his brother was killed.

After the war Dubček was a loyal and hard-working party member who rose through the ranks to become the secretary of the Central Committee of the Communist Party in Slovakia in 1962. When party leader Antonín Novotný resigned in January 1968, Dubček was unanimously elected by the Central Committee to replace him, becoming the first Slovak to head Czechoslovakia's Communist Party.

Dubček was chosen because he had no enemies and would offend no one. Some politicians thought he would be easy to manipulate, but they quickly discovered otherwise. Once in power, Dubček began to initiate far-ranging reforms in the communist system to give this nation, in his words, "socialism with a human face."

Under Dubček's liberal rule the economy experimented with a free-market system, trade was initiated with the West, censorship ended, and the arts and intellectualism were encouraged. The "Prague Spring," however, proved to be a short season: On August 21, 1968, the Soviet invasion of Czechoslovakia began, and Dubček was taken to Moscow. He returned home a week later a broken man. The reforms soon ended, and in 1970 Dubček was expelled from the party. He lived in obscurity in Bratislava, the Slovak capital, for nearly two decades.

When communism finally fell, however, the new leaders of the country remembered his achievement and recalled him to Prague, where he served in the government of Václav Havel until his sudden death in 1992, at age 70, resulting from a car accident.

private as well as state businesses. Czechoslovakia increased its trade and dialogue with the Western nations. All these reforms were part of Dubček's goal of creating "socialism with a human face." After 20 years of the long, dark winter of communist suppression, Dubček had opened the window and let in some sunlight and fresh air to his country. People called it the Prague Spring.

Just as Stalin had feared that Yugoslavia's break with the Soviet Union would inspire other countries to do the same, Brezhnev feared the liberalization of Czechoslovakia would encourage the governments of Poland, Hungary, and other Soviet satellites to enact reforms. Dubček insisted that he had no such motive in mind and that what worked for the Czechs would not work elsewhere, but Brezhnev remained skeptical.

In truth, what Dubček was establishing in Czechoslovakia was the kind of socialism that the Soviets had given lip service to for years—a form of government where the needs of people came first. But the hypocrisy of the communist system, in which a privileged few held absolute power over the masses, could not stand being shown for the sham it was. In that sense, Brezhnev had good reason to fear the Prague Spring.

Then in May 1968 Czech writer Ludvík Vaculík (b. 1926) published a manifesto that was like a gauntlet flung down before the Soviets. In *The 2,000 Words,* which thousands of Czechs and Slovaks signed, Vaculík condemned the Communist Party for a betrayal of trust: "The inconstant line of the leadership," wrote Vaculík, "changed the party from a political party and an ideological alliance into a power organization that became very attractive to egotists avid for rule, calculating cowards and unprincipled people."

Brezhnev was aghast. He ordered Dubček to publicly condemn the manifesto. When he did not, the Czech president was told to come to Moscow; Dubček politely declined the invitation. The two men met a few weeks later, but neither would budge on his stand. Dubček returned home, convinced that Brezhnev would not attempt to interfere with his reforms.

But at 10:30 P.M. on Tuesday, August 20, 1968, Soviet warplanes landed at Prague's Ruzyne Airport. Armed Soviet soldiers effectively took over the airport. Within hours more than 200,000 troops from five Warsaw Pact countries descended on Czechoslovakia. By dawn Soviet tanks were rolling into the capital. The Prague Spring was over, and a chilling Soviet winter was returning to the land.

Dubček and several high officials in his government were arrested and flown to Moscow in handcuffs. They were questioned and put in prison. Brezhnev hoped the Czech people would greet the soldiers as liberators; instead, they saw them for what they were—invaders. A Czech journalist depicted the grim scene in Prague's Wenceslas Square the afternoon of the first full day of the Soviet takeover:

> Over Venohradska Street the smoke from burning houses still rises into the sky. We pass a smoke-smudged youth carrying a sad souvenir—the shell of an 85-mm gun. The fountain below the museum splashes quietly, just as it did yesterday, as if nothing had happened, but when you raise your eyes to the facade of the museum, you freeze in your steps. Against the dark background shine hundreds of white spots, as if evil birds had pecked at the facade. . . . "Soldiers, go home! Quickly!" implores an inscription in Russian fastened to the pedestal of St. Wenseslaus's statue. And below, around the statue, silently sit the young and the old. Saint Wenseslaus is decorated with Czechoslovak flags. . . . People sit dejectedly on the pedestal. On the street corner, small groups of people listen to transistor radios.

Nearly 200 Czechs and Slovaks were killed during the invasion, and hundreds were wounded in clashes with troops. The Western nations, including the United States, condemned the invasion. So did several Communist countries, including Yugoslavia, China, and North Vietnam. But no one tried to stop it. The Czechs were left to deal with their tragedy as best they could. Dubček returned home after a few days, a sad and broken man. He remained president for the time being—his popularity with the people made it difficult for even Brezhnev to remove him—but the reforms he spearheaded came to an end.

The despair and frustration the Czech people felt was dramatically symbolized by Jan Palach, a 21-year-old student. On a cold day in mid-January 1969 Palach drenched himself with gasoline and set himself on fire as an act of protest. Although the authorities moved his body to an unknown location, his memory would not be forgotten. Palach was hailed by the people as a martyr to Soviet tyranny.

In April, Dubček was replaced as first secretary by his colleague Gustáv Husák (1913–91). Husák, a victim of Stalin, had learned his lesson and embraced the party line; he would remain in power for 20 years. Dubček was demoted to ambassador to Turkey and eventually went home to Bratislava, the Slovak capital. He took a job as a mechanic for the Forestry Department to support his family and remained in obscurity until he retired in 1981.

Years of Protest, Years of Change

Husák and the hard-liners in Prague might control the country, but they could not push the economy forward. In the 1970s economic stagnation grew worse, and inflation soared. Students and intellectuals again led demonstrations and protests. One of the leaders of the protest movement was Czech playwright Václav Havel (see boxed biography, Chapter 3). During the relaxation of censorship in the 1960s Havel had become celebrated for his dark comedies that satirized the Communist bureaucracy. With the end of the Prague Spring, Havel became a nonperson, his works forbidden to be performed or published. In January 1977 he helped found the human rights movement Charter 77. The organization gave a focus to Czech resistance and was a real threat to the Communists. One Charter 77 leader, Jan Patocka, died mysteriously after being detained by the police. Havel was arrested in October 1979, charged with "subversion," and sentenced to four and one-half years at hard labor. He was released 10 months early due to ill health.

In 1985 a new leader came to power in the Soviet Union. Like Dubček in Czechoslovakia, Mikhail Gorbachev (b. 1931) brought reform and change to the rigid communist system. Gorbachev's emphasis on economic reform, a reduction in the military, and the relaxation of censorship left hard-liners like Husák and the Communist leaders in other Eastern bloc countries suddenly out in the cold. In December 1987 Husák resigned as party leader. However, the stubborn Communists refused to cave in and replaced him with the even more conservative Miloš Jakeš.

On August 20, 1988–the 20th anniversary of the Soviet invasion— 10,000 demonstrators marched in Prague. Police attacked the demonstrators and made arrests. But the unrest was far greater in neighboring

Communist countries. The Solidarity trade-union movement in Poland had forced the Communists to the negotiation table. Free elections were in the offing in Poland. Communists, who could no longer count on

Many Czechs and Slovaks reacted to the Soviet invasion of their country with courageous resistance. Here a demonstrator defiantly holds the Czech national flag before a Soviet tank in Prague's city center. (AP Photo)

support of the Soviet Union, were being thrown out of Hungary and Bulgaria. By November of 1989, new democratic governments were firmly in place in Poland, Hungary, and East Germany, where the Berlin Wall that had separated communist East Germany from capitalist West Germany for nearly three decades was being torn down. The time for change had come for Czechoslovakia as well. The question was, What form would that change take?

NOTES

p. 15 "'Peace for our time.'" *World Book,* Vol. 3 (Chicago: World Book, Inc., 1986), p. 284.

p. 16 "'The air rages . . .'" Lawrence L. Langer, ed., *Art from the Ashes: A Holocaust Anthology* (Oxford, U.K.: Oxford University Press, 1995), p. 67.

p. 17 "'I went to Moscow . . .'" Dan Riley, *The People's Almanac #3* (New York: Bantam, 1981), p. 6.

p. 18 "'Sitting in a yoga position . . .'" Riley, *The People's Almanac #3*, p. 9.

pp. 19–20 "'When the eleven condemned . . .'" Tad Szulc, *Czechoslovakia since World War II* (New York: Viking, 1971), p. 105.

p. 22 "'It's been a hard life, . . .'" *Connecticut Post*, November 8, 1992, n.p.

pp. 22–23 "'Socialism with a human face.'" Dubček, Alexander. *Hope Dies Last: The Autobiography of the Leader of the Prague Spring* (New York: Kodansha International, 1993), back cover.

p. 23 "'The inconstant line . . .'" Ina Navazelskis, *Alexander Dubček* (New York: Chelsea House, 1990), p. 87.

p. 24 "'Over Venohradska Street . . .'" Robert Littell, *The Czech Black Book* (New York: Praeger, 1969), pp. 49–50.

3

THE VELVET REVOLUTION, THE VELVET DIVORCE, AND THE VELVET RECOVERY (1989–PRESENT)

As the authoritarian world that they had known for 40 years crumbled around them, the Communist leaders of Czechoslovakia shut their eyes and carried on. Pressured by his people, who clamored for freedom, and the Soviets, who urged immediate reform, President Jakeš loosened restrictions on travel and allowed more freedom of worship and less censorship. On the political front, however, nothing changed.

"The leadership here is dead, only waiting to be carried away," dissident Jiří Dienstbier (b. 1937) told the *New York Times* in November 1989. "The party's only alternative to the status quo is to open up the system, but they know that once they open it up, they are doomed."

The end, delayed for so long, came with shuddering speed. On November 17, 1989, the capital city saw the largest political demonstration since the Prague Spring of 1968. The demonstrators, at first mostly students and intellectuals, were brutally attacked by the police. This gained them the sympathy and support of the workers. Soon, the crowds in Prague swelled to more than 200,000. As the demonstrations continued, opposition groups, including Charter 77, met to form one large organization—Civic

Forum—"as a spokesman on behalf of that part of the Czechoslovak public which is increasingly critical of the existing Czechoslovak leadership." Desperately losing ground, Jakeš and his cohorts agreed to hold talks with Civic Forum and its leader, Václav Havel.

On the sixth day of the demonstrations, a voice from the past lent his weight and authority to the cries for the resignation of the Communist leadership. Alexander Dubček, now 68 years old, gave his first public speech in 21 years to an audience of 2,000 Slovaks in Bratislava and called for the formation of a new, freely elected government. In a message read later to the people of Prague, he expressed his solidarity with them and his desire to stand with them in Wenceslas Square.

Three days later, on November 24, the Communist leadership resigned, but new Communists replaced them, led by Karel Urbánek, party leader of Bohemia. "The new leadership is a trick that was meant to confuse," said Havel. "The power remains in or is passing into the hands of the neo-Stalinists."

The following day, a Saturday, the demonstrators in Prague numbered 800,000. A two-hour general strike was set for Monday at noon by the protest leaders. When the time came, millions of Czech and Slovak workers left their jobs and walked into the streets. For two hours, the entire country shut down. Only hospitals, nursing homes, and a few businesses remained open. The people stood and cried in the streets of joy. After decades of frustration, they knew their time had finally come.

"Before this, I was afraid of what would come next," confessed a 21-year-old student. "Our professor told us recently that our country was turning into a memorial display of Communism. But now we have taken our own way."

The final blow came, ironically, from the Soviets. Mikhail Gorbachev declared the 1968 reform movement of Dubček had been "a process of democratization, renewal and humanization of society." The Russians not only officially condemned the invasion but also seriously considered the withdrawal of remaining Soviet troops from Czechoslovakia. On December 7, Ladislav Adamec, one of the most moderate of the Communist leaders, resigned as prime minister. His replacement, the Slovak Marián Calfa, was ready to negotiate for a transition of power. Three days later, on International Human Rights Day, a coalition government took power, with the Communists in the minority. Dubček was

Some 200,000 people gather in Prague's Wenceslas Square on November 20, 1989, to participate in one of the largest protest rallies ever held in the city. The banner reads Svobodne volby, *meaning "free elections."* (AP Photo/Peter de Jong)

named chairman of the national Federal Assembly, and on December 29, 1989, this body unanimously elected Václav Havel as the country's first noncommunist president in 40 years. Havel said he had no intentions of becoming a politician and promised to step down when a new president was elected the following year in the country's first free elections since 1946.

The Czech "revolution" was seen as something of a miracle abroad. After years of repression, terror, and death, the Czechs had ended Communist rule bloodlessly, without a single loss of life. The transfer of power in Prague was peaceful and smooth—so smooth that the world called it "the Velvet Revolution." Few realized the end of communism would quickly lead to the end of Czechoslovakia itself.

Reign of the Philosopher King

Václav Havel cut a strange figure as president of his country. A man of the people, he shunned the trappings of his office in Hradčany Castle,

VÁCLAV HAVEL (b. 1936)

The first president of the Czech Republic was born into one of Prague's wealthiest families. His father was a property owner and restaurateur; his uncle owned the largest motion picture studio in Czechoslovakia. All that changed in 1948 when the Communists took over the country. The new government nationalized business and industry, and overnight the Havels lost everything. The future playwright was denied a university education and was forced to earn a living as a worker in a chemical laboratory.

Determined to get an education, Havel enrolled in night school to earn his high school diploma and drove a taxi by day to pay his tuition. Turned down time and again by the university, he took a job as a stagehand at an avant-garde theater in Prague. He progressed from stagehand to electrician, secretary, literary manager, and finally playwright. His plays, with their double-talk and absurd humor, mercilessly satirized the Communist system. In 1968, during the Prague Spring, Havel was allowed to visit the first American production of one of his plays in New York City. It was named the best off-Broadway foreign play of the season.

But with the Soviet invasion in August, Havel once again experienced a complete turnabout. Overnight, Czechoslovakia's most prominent playwright was a nonperson: His plays were banned from the stage and his books forbidden to be published or sold. Havel fought back by becoming a full-time dissident. In the 1970s he was arrested repeatedly, jailed twice, and forced to make a meager living by stacking barrels in a brewery for $50 a week. Continuing his role as a spokesperson for the human rights movement, he was arrested in October 1979, charged with "subversion," and sentenced to four and one-half years at hard labor. During his imprisonment Havel almost died from pneumonia, complicated by a lung abscess. The government offered him freedom if he would only request a pardon. Havel refused. Nonetheless, his sentence was suspended due to ill health in early 1983, 10 months short of its completion.

Five years later the Communist government collapsed and Václav Havel, his country's leading dissident, was the unanimous choice to head the new government. He accepted the honor, determined to make the lives of his people better. "Dear friends, I promise you I will not betray your confidence," he told them.

But the leaders of the two factions in Czechoslovakia appeared to disappoint him. As Czech prime minister Václav Klaus and Slovak prime minister Vladimír Mečiar worked out a plan to divide their country into two separate nations, Havel resigned from the presidency in disgust. With the establishment of the Czech Republic in January 1993, he agreed to run again for president and was elected leader of the new nation.

In 1998 Havel was reelected to a second term as president. Over the next five years many Czechs criticized him for his extravagant spending; his unpopular second wife, actress Dagmar Veckrnova; and his lack of a strong, political agenda for the nation.

When he stepped down as president in January 2003, feelings about his 13 years in office were mixed, but many acknowledged Havel's uniqueness as a public figure. "I'm sure we will miss him, because he was bigger than Czech politics," noted journalist Tomáš Klvaňa. "He aimed at concepts that cannot be discussed in television sound bites."

In 1989 creative artist, deep thinker, playwright, and dissident Václav Havel made an unlikely presidential candidate for anywhere else perhaps but in Czechoslovakia.
(AP Photo)

the traditional home of Czech rulers. He appointed intellectuals, fellow writers, and artists to his Council of Advisers and sometimes rode around the halls of the castle on a child's scooter. But for all this Havel took his job seriously. He set about not only reforming the government and establishing democratic freedom and personal rights but also transforming the planned economy of the Communists to a free-market system where people could run their own businesses and farms.

In February 1990 Havel visited the United States for the first time as president. In an address before the joint houses of the U.S. Congress, he spoke eloquently about his people and his mission:

> . . . The salvation of our world can be found only in the human heart, in the power of humans to reflect, in human meekness and responsibility.
>
> Without a global revolution in the sphere of human consciousness, nothing will change for the better in the sphere of our being as humans, and the catastrophe towards which this world is headed—be it ecological, social, demographic, or a general breakdown of civilization—will be unavoidable. If we are no longer threatened by world war or by the danger of absurd mountains of nuclear weapons blowing up the world, this does not mean that we have finally won. This is actually far from being a final victory. . . .
>
> I shall close by repeating what I said at the beginning: history has accelerated. I believe that once again it will be the human mind that perceives this acceleration, comprehends its shape, and transforms its own words into deeds.

Both at home and abroad, Havel was seen as a national hero, and he decided to run for a full term as president in elections held in the spring of 1990. He won by a large majority. The Civic Forum, in coalition with another opposition group, Public Against Violence, took 56 percent of the seats in the Federal Assembly, winning out over 20 other parties. The Communist Party, interestingly enough, was the second biggest winner, taking 47 of the 300 seats in the assembly. The country was in a celebratory mood, but under the goodwill and joy, old ethnic divisions and rivalries were beginning to fray the fabric of the Velvet Revolution.

Slovakia Wants to Be Free

In April 1990 Slovak sociologist Fedor Gál was asked in an interview what he thought of the chances of "separatist tendencies" in his region. "It's absurd to think that a small, angry nation like Slovakia has any prospects whatever . . ." he replied. "I'd very much like to be able to label these separatists 'fringe extremists.'"

But by 1992 the extremists seemed to be gaining ground. Vladimír Mečiar (b. 1942), a former Slovak Communist and self-avowed populist, had emerged as the main spokesman for the separatists and head of a new political party, the Movement for a Democratic Slovakia. Mečiar argued convincingly that the Slovaks were suffering economically far more than the Czechs in the transition from a planned communist economy to a free-market one. Long bolstered up by the Soviets, the Slovak economy plummeted with their withdrawal from Czechoslovakian affairs, and unemployment in the region soared to 12 percent. Less industrialized than the Czech lands, Slovakia could not manage for itself in the shifting marketplace. Largely rural, its agricultural economy was outmoded and ill equipped to deal with the free market.

Mečiar's campaign touched a sensitive nerve with all Slovaks. The resentment they felt toward their better-educated and more affluent Czech cousins had deep roots. Ever since the formation of Czechoslovakia in 1918, the Czechs had politically dominated the Slovaks, denying them full representation in the government and most often telling them what to do. This bossy side of the Czech character was matched by the stubborn, proud side of the Slovaks. After more than 70 years of Czech and Communist domination, the Slovaks were ready for a change. Now, with the bonds of communism broken, Mečiar was calling for independence for Slovakia. He threatened to block Havel's reelection as president by running against him in the upcoming national elections of June 1992. If he won control of the Slovak Parliament, Mečiar threatened to call for a referendum on the issue of separation. Havel considered Mečiar and his party as opportunists out to gain power for themselves. He claimed that such a split between Czechs and Slovaks would lead to political chaos and urged citizens of both ethnic groups not to cast their vote "for people for whom power is more important than the fate of the nation. . . ."

In an election in which 90 percent of Czechoslovaks turned out to vote, Mečiar's party took one-third of the Slovak vote, while close to half of all Czech votes were cast for the right-wing coalition centered around Finance Minister Václav Klaus (b. 1941), head of the new Civic Democratic Party (ODS). The former Communists trailed in third place with 13 percent of the vote. The political lines had been drawn. Klaus, who became prime minister shortly after, saw the future of the country moving swiftly away from socialism to a free-market economy. Mečiar, elected prime minister of Slovakia, saw this rush to democracy as devastating to his country's economy and refused to accept Klaus's policies.

The Velvet Divorce

On July 17, 1992, the Slovak National Council adopted a declaration of sovereignty in a vote of 113 to 24. Three days later President Havel resigned, refusing to preside over the dissolution of his country.

Czech prime minister Klaus met with his Slovak counterpart, Mečiar, and the two men negotiated what a short time before most of their compatriots thought unthinkable—the dissolution of their state. On November 25, the Federal Assembly of Czechoslovakia voted the split to go into effect at midnight on December 31. While many Czechs and Slovaks did not feel as repulsed as Havel did over the division, only a few enthusiastically supported it. In a *New York Times* poll taken in the fall of 1992, only 37 percent of Slovaks and 36 percent of Czechs said they would vote for the split in a referendum, yet more than 80 percent saw such a split as inevitable and were resigned to it.

Like the Velvet Revolution, the Velvet Divorce was peaceful and completed with little disruption. With only 50,000 Czechs living in Slovakia and 300,000 Slovaks in the Czech Republic, there was no great uprooting of populations. All territorial claims were dismissed; land was the property of the republic it was located in. Special commissions were set up to divide other property on the basis of population size and a ratio of 2 (Czech Republic) to 1 (Slovak Republic). Military personnel were allowed to serve the republic to which they felt most loyal.

With the split the government of Prime Minister Klaus moved its economic reform forward with more speed. Havel reentered the political arena and ran for the presidency of the Czech Republic. He easily beat his two opponents and was sworn into office on February 2, 1993. Politically more liberal than Klaus, Havel was often at odds with his prime minister.

As Klaus attended to the economy and internal affairs, Havel reached out to strengthen bonds with new friends and former enemies abroad. In August 1993 Russian president Boris Yeltsin (b. 1931) visited Prague and met with Havel to sign a treaty with the new republic on the 25th anniversary of the Soviet invasion. The new treaty, Havel said, provided the "psychological and political climate" for closer relations between the two countries. Yeltsin, for his part, condemned the 1968 invasion and laid flowers on a memorial to Czech women shot by Soviet soldiers while waiting for a tram in Prague during the invasion.

In January 1994 U.S. president Bill Clinton (b. 1946) met with Havel and other leaders of eastern Europe. While Havel's relationship with the United States remained a positive one, he expressed frustration over the United States's refusal to allow his country into the North Atlantic Treaty Organization (NATO, an organization formed in 1949 composed mostly of western European countries and the United States for mutual defense if any one nation is attacked), which many Czechs believed would strengthen ties with the West and stave off any future threat from Russia.

During 1994 the privatization of state-owned companies continued at an accelerated rate. Klaus had hit upon a unique way to entice the public to become a part of this process: The government issued booklets of vouchers that adults could buy for $35 and use either to bid for shares in independent state companies or to invest in new mutual funds.

While the program largely succeeded, the prime minister's critics pointed out that many of the newly privatized companies carried large debts held by state banks, a glaring conflict of interest that could upset the economy and lead to bankruptcy. At the end of 1994 the head of the voucher program was arrested for carrying $286,000 in a suitcase and was charged with bribery. Klaus later reassigned the man to a job in the tax office.

Called by some "the toughest leader of Post-Communism's biggest success story," Klaus continued to stir up controversy as he moved his country down the road to capitalism. He proposed that students pay fees for a university education, something never considered under the

Communists. "Every investment costs something," he explained. "If you want to invest, you have to pay something first. Then you get your money back."

To illustrate his point further, Klaus questioned the social security program in the Czech Republic and introduced legislation to raise the retirement age for men from 62 to 65 and for women from 55 to 62.

The Coalition Collapses

Parliamentary elections held in June 1996 saw a serious weakening in the government coalition. Voters were growing dissatisfied with Klaus's autocratic rule and the threat he posed to many of the social services put in place under the Communists. As a result many Czechs voted for the left-of-center Social Democratic Party (CSSD). The government narrowly lost its majority in the Chamber of Deputies, Parliament's lower house, and Klaus was forced to form a new minority government in order to remain in office.

In November, elections were held for a new upper house of the Parliament, the 81-member Senate, provided for in the 1993 constitution. The coalition regained some of its strength, winning a majority of seats, but by spring 1997 the Klaus government was again in trouble. Klaus's refusal to deal with underlying problems of the transition from a state-run economy to a free-market one led to rising deficits and falling growth rates. Another government financial scandal and summer flooding that devastated a third of the country only made matters worse.

By November the coalition collapsed, and Klaus was forced to resign as prime minister. An interim government was appointed in January 1998 headed by Josef Tošovský, who later became governor of the Czech National Bank.

Havel was elected the same year to a second five-year term as president but by a narrow margin. His popularity with the people was starting to fade as well. He often stood above the political fray as a moral force and his nation's conscience, but his aloofness did not help solve the nation's problems, and many people accused him of wasting the political capital he could have used to effect change.

The Social Democrats Take Over

In May 1998 there was some good news for the problem-ridden nation. The U.S. Senate at last approved the acceptance of the Czech Republic, Poland, and Hungary as full members in NATO. The Czechs' alignment with the West seemed all but complete, but curiously the Czech people were less enthusiastic about belonging to NATO than the Poles and Hungarians were. Only 50 percent of Czechs, according to one poll, favored NATO membership.

The pains and uncertainty of transition to a free-market economy were beginning to be felt in the Czech Republic, and people were casting a fond eye back to the more familiar ways of the communist past. In the June 1998 election the CSSD, offering less pain and slower change, won a majority of nearly 33 percent of the vote, with the ODS coming in second place with 28 percent. The two rival parties agreed to a new minority government run by the Social Democrats. CSSD party leader Miloš Zeman was appointed prime minister.

The new government's more measured approach to economic and social change pleased many Czechs, but there were signs of continuing corruption. Even more unsettling were charges of a government assault on the rights of a free press and media. The government fired the news and programming heads of the government-supported public Czech Television, and a well-known and outspoken news commentator with Radio Free Europe was let go by government-sponsored Czech Radio. Others journalists and broadcasters who criticized the government were in danger of losing their jobs. "This is a semiliberal corrupt regime," declared Jiří Pehe, director of New York University's Prague branch, "and the antidemocratic attitudes that were bred into people during Communism are re-emerging."

A New President

The growing tide of criticism against the Social Democrats gave Klaus and the ODS hope. They ran a hard race against the government in the June 2002 elections. Klaus questioned Czech efforts to join the European Union (EU), a group of 15 nations that traded with one another, and called for big cuts in taxes. The Social Democrats campaigned on slow but steady economic growth and an increase in spending on social services. On Election Day, the CSSD was returned to power with 30 percent of the vote to the ODS's 24 percent. The Czech Communist Party ran a strong third place with 19 percent of the vote.

Vladimír Špidla, (b. 1951) a historian, was appointed the new prime minister, replacing Zeman. In his acceptance speech Špidla focused on pursuing a socialist agenda and strengthening ties with the West. "We strive to create a modern welfare state and prepare for joining the European Union," he said.

The twice-defeated Klaus, in a surprising move, ran for president in early 2003 as Havel stepped down after 13 years in office. The presidential race went through three rounds of parliamentary voting before Klaus emerged the unexpected victor, beating out the handpicked Socialist candidate. Špidla and his government were stunned by Klaus's victory.

A number of CSSD members secretly supported Klaus and would like to abandon the current government coalition and form a new one with the Civic

A historian by profession, Prime Minister Vladimir Špidla has had a difficult time keeping his party together since his 2002 election. (Courtesy Embassy of the Czech Republic in Washington, D.C.)

Democrats. This division within the CSSD has called Špidla's leadership into question.

In a countermove in May 2003, Špidla dismissed Jiří Rusnok, the trade and industry minister and one of the most vocal members of opposition within the party. Whether Špidla and his supporters can again unite their government and bring positive change to the Czech Republic remains to be seen.

NOTES

p. 29 "'The leadership here is dead, . . .'" Bernard Gwertzman and Michael T. Kaufman, *The Collapse of Communism* (New York: Times Books, 1990), p. 226.

p. 30 "'as a spokesman . . .'" Gale Stokes, *The Walls Came Tumbling Down: The Collapse of Communism in Eastern Europe* (New York: Oxford University Press, 1993), p. 156.

p. 30 "'The new leadership . . .'" Gwertzman and Kaufman, *The Collapse of Communism*, p. 237.

p. 30 "'Before this, I was afraid . . .'" Gwertzman and Kaufman, *The Collapse of Communism*, pp. 265–266.

p. 32 "'Dear friends, . . .'" Gwertzman and Kaufman, *The Collapse of Communism*, p. 344.

p. 33 "'I'm sure we will miss him . . .'" *New York Times*, January 25, 2003, p. A3.

p. 34 "'The salvation of our world . . .'" Václav Havel, "Address to a Joint Session of the United States Congress," *After the Velvet Revolution* (London: Freedom House, 1991), pp. 78, 80.

p. 35 "'separatist tendencies' . . . 'It's absurd . . .'" Fedor Gál, "Slovakia's Problems and Prospects," *After the Velvet Revolution* (London: Freedom House, 1991), pp. 231–232.

p. 35 "'for people for whom . . .'" *New York Times*, June 6, 1992, n.p.

p. 37 "'psychological and political climate,'" *New York Times*, August 27, 1993, p. A3.

p. 37 "'the toughest leader . . .'" Jane Perlez, "The First in the Velvet Glove," *New York Times Magazine*, July 16, 1995, p. 17.

p. 38 "'Every investment costs something . . .'" Jane Perlez, *New York Times Magazine*, p. 17.

p. 39 "'This is a semiliberal corrupt regime . . .'" *New York Times*, November 18, 2001, p. A18.

p. 40 "'We strive to create . . .'" *New York Times*, June 16, 2002, p. 4.

PART II
Czech Republic Today

4

GOVERNMENT

It is not surprising that democracy has taken firmer root in the soil of the Czech Republic than in that of any of its neighbors in eastern Europe. No other country in the region has had as much experience with this form of government. The nearly two-decade administration of Tomáš Masaryk was the shining example of democracy in Central Europe between the world wars. The liberal socialist experiment of the Dubček government in 1968 challenged 20 years of Communist rule. Although it was quickly crushed, it was not forgotten. The intellectual-led human rights movement of the 1980s was driven by democratic ideals and a burning desire for a free and open society.

The government that was founded by the Czechs and Slovaks in the wake of communism's downfall was one anchored in this rich democratic past. But the "Velvet Recovery," as it was called by its chief architect, Prime Minister Václav Klaus, was not all that it appeared to be. It was a pragmatic mix of shock-therapy economics and soft-pedaled socialism. The arch-capitalist Klaus did not burn all his bridges with the communist past. Subsidies for electricity and heating continued, as did rent controls. Workers were kept employed in state-owned factories, although they had little work to do. By keeping the safety nets of socialism in place, Klaus largely avoided the painful symptoms—soaring inflation, high unemployment, and a lower standard of living—that had accompanied the transition from a planned economy to a free-market one elsewhere in eastern Europe.

Václav Klaus is the Czech Republic's second president. His election was a surprise to many and a serious blow to the rival Social Democratic government. (Courtesy Embassy of the Czech Republic in Washington, D.C.)

But Klaus's refusal to face the harder realities of this transition from a planned to free-market economy finally caught up with him. In 1997 the Czech Republic experienced a financial crisis and recession that sent the economy plummeting. The voters turned to the more left-wing Social Democratic Party, led by Miloš Zeman, one of Klaus's severest critics. Zeman vowed to save the social services the people had known under communism and slow down the transition to a free market.

The Zeman government had its problems, too, particularly in the area of censorship and personal rights. However, the economy rebounded in 2001, helping Zeman to win reelection in 2002. Klaus's Civic Democratic Party failed to retake power coming in second in the elections, but in early 2003 Klaus ran for president and won. It was a devastating blow for the government of the Social Democrats.

The Prime Minister

While Klaus extends considerable influence as president, he does not run the government. His role as head of state is partly ceremonial, although he does represent his nation at home and abroad. He is also the

VÁCLAV KLAUS (b. 1941)

Aloof, autocratic, and a firm advocate of Western free enterprise, Václav Klaus has the survival skills of a consummate politician. The first prime minister of the Czech Republic and its second president, Klaus was born in Prague on June 19, 1941. He studied international economic relations and trade at the Prague School of Economics, from which he graduated in 1963. For the next seven years he worked as a researcher at the Academy of Sciences' Institute of Economics until he was fired for his Western political views. Like his longtime political rival, Václav Havel, he had to work his way back up the career ladder through menial jobs, eventually becoming a member of the Institute for Economic Forecasting in the Academy of Sciences in 1988.

Klaus joined the Civic Forum during the Velvet Revolution and quickly became its leader and chief spokesman. When the forum split in 1991, Klaus helped found the Civic Democratic Party. He served as finance minister in the Czechoslovak government from late 1988 to mid-1992. When his party won the general election of 1992, he became prime minister.

After his resignation in November 1997 amid financial scandals and a crumbling economy, Klaus was elected to the Chamber of Deputies where he served as speaker from 1998 to 2002. When President Havel heard of his ambitions to succeed him as president, Havel considered stalling the formation of a new government to keep Klaus out of office if he won the election.

While Klaus softened his campaign style to become president, his views are as opinionated as ever. He is skeptical about the Czech Republic joining the EU and sees it as a move toward a centralized European state in which his country may lose its political and economic independence. Just as Havel often proved a thorn in Klaus's side as president, so President Klaus may be a constant irritant to the Social Democrats.

commander-in-chief of the armed forces and appoints government officials and judges.

The prime minister, on the other hand, runs the government with his cabinet, which consists of two deputy prime ministers and individual ministers in a number of areas. He is appointed by the president at the suggestion of the speaker of the legislature. While both houses of Parliament elect the president to a five-year-term, the prime minister remains in power until his party loses the nation's confidence or is voted out of office.

Since July 2002 the Czech prime minister has been Vladimír Špidla. Špidla was vice chairman of the CSSD before his appointment, but he is not a career politician. He majored in history and prehistory at Charles University in Prague and later was an archaeologist at the District Museum of Jindřichův Hradec. He became Vice chairman of the District National Committee responsible for education, health care, and social affairs in 1990. A founding member of the CSSD, Špidla was the party's spokesman for labor and social affairs from 1996.

Špidla faced many challenges in his first year as prime minister. Division within the Social Democratic Party over the future of the government coalition has brought his leadership into question.

The Legislative and Judicial Branches

The legislative branch of government, called Parliament, is made up of two separate houses, not unlike the U.S. Congress. Under the new constitution of January 1, 1993, the lower house, the Chamber of Deputies, consists of 200 members, who are elected for four-year terms and proportionally represent their districts. The Senate, established in 1997 under the constitution, has 81 members, who are elected for six-year terms, one per district. One-third of the Senate is elected every two years.

The judiciary branch of government, established a year and a half before the legislative branch was, consists of four kinds of courts—civil, criminal, commercial, and administrative.

Criminal and civil cases are usually handled by district courts ruled by a judge and two associate judges. Associate judges are elected for four-year terms. Regional courts in the larger cities deal with cases pertaining to commercial and trade laws. Cases can be appealed to higher courts up to the country's Supreme Court. Chairman and deputy chairmen of the Supreme Court are appointed by the president for 10-year terms. There is also a 15-member Constitutional Court that interprets the constitution in certain cases. Its members are also appointed by the president. There is no death penalty in the Czech Republic.

Administrative courts handle cases appealed by citizens who question the legality of decisions of state institutions. Commercial courts examine disputes in business matters.

Local Government

The Czech Republic is divided into 13 administrative regions, or *kraje*, and the capital city, Prague. The administrative regions are Jihočeský Kraj, Jihomoravský Kraj, Karlovarský Kraj, Královéhradecký Kraj, Liberecký Kraj, Moravskoslezský Kraj, Olomoucký Kraj, Pardubický Kraj, Plzeňský, Středočeský Kraj, Ústecký Kraj, Vysočina, and Zlínský Kraj.

District bureaus have replaced the national committees that once ran regional and local government under the communist system. These bureaus have the power to raise local taxes. They oversee the building and maintaining of roadways, public health, utilities, and the school system. Nevertheless, their power is strictly limited by the national government.

"They [the Czechs] have democracy at a macro-level, but there's a lack of decentralization of political power," points out Stephen Heinz of the Institute for East-West Studies in Prague. "But in this country, which was a democratic country with a long history of democracy, it's not such an alarming situation as it might be elsewhere in the region."

The Armed Forces

Under the Communists, Czechoslovakia had a 200,000-strong military force on active duty. While large, the armed forces were poorly trained with few professional skills. After independence and the split with Slovakia, the Czech Republic reduced its armed forces to less than half.

Upon joining NATO in March 1999, the move to reduce and streamline the military accelerated. With NATO's help the Czechs are working to raise the standard of professionalism until it meets the level of other NATO forces. The present goal is to have a 35,000-strong army by the year 2007.

The two military areas where the Czech Republic is strongest are the identifying and detection of chemical and biological weapons and the gathering of electronic intelligence. These have proven to be especially useful skills in the ongoing war against terrorism.

In March 2002, in the wake of the September 11, 2001, terrorist attacks on New York City and Washington, D.C., 252 Czech soldiers went to Kuwait to be part of the Enduring Freedom mission. They were later joined by soldiers from neighboring Slovakia.

While the Czech army is making good progress, the nation's air defense is not faring as well. Financial problems prevented the Czech government from buying 24 supersonic jet fighters in 2003. Two options for defending its air space are turning it over to outside NATO forces or working out a joint air defense with Slovakia.

Whatever the future holds for defense, the Czech Republic takes its commitment to NATO seriously. "Whenever the interest of the alliance is threatened you are there and ready to help," said Jan Vana, head of the army's department for strategic planning. "And it is better to protect the interests of the alliance outside of its territory. Prevention is the key word."

Foreign Policy

Czech foreign policy is largely determined by two major alliances— NATO and the EU, of which the country should be a full member by 2004.

While a certain percentage of Czechs had reservations about joining NATO in 1999, they were able to put them aside for the good of their country. Similar reservations about joining the EU have been expressed by members of the ODS and the Communist Party. However, a growing majority of the population favors membership. The movement to join the EU has been a positive force in Czech affairs. To meet the EU's requirements, the government has had to work harder to clean up political corruption, environmental pollution, and crime (see Chapter 10).

As a member of NATO, the Czech Republic has forged stronger ties with western Europe and particularly the United States. During the U.S.-led war in Afghanistan in 2002 against the repressive Taliban government, Czech doctors and orderlies established a field hospital in Kabul, the Afghan capital, that remained in operation for six months.

Loyalty to NATO, however, has its limits. When rumors spread in spring 2003 that the United States might move some of its military bases to the Czech Republic and other Eastern bloc NATO members, many Czechs were not pleased. They feared the establishment of these bases in their country would make it easier for the United States to draw them into an Iraqi-like conflict. "I will do all that I can to make the realization of this idea difficult," said Vladimír Laštůvka, chairman of the Chamber of Deputies Foreign Committee.

Closer to home, the Czechs are patching up their differences with the Slovaks. Bitter and angry over the imbalance of divided resources when the two nations split in 1993, Slovakia has been appeased by a recent financial settlement made by the Czech Republic.

NOTES

p. 49 "'They [the Czechs] have democracy . . .'" *Christian Science Monitor,* May 24, 1995, p. 8.

p. 50 "'Whenever the interest . . .'" Daniela Lazarova, Radio Prague. Available on-line. URL: http://www.radio.cz/en/article/35075. Downloaded June 5, 2003.

p. 51 "'I will do . . .'" Kevin Livingston, *Prague Post.* Available on-line. URL: http://www.praguepost.com/P03/2003/Art/0508/news1.php. Downloaded May 12, 2003.

5
RELIGION

In a country where religion has historically played a leading role since Saints Cyril and Methodius first introduced Christianity in about A.D. 700, the Czech Republic is today a surprisingly irreligious nation. While nearly 40 percent of the population is Roman Catholic, an equal percentage profess no religious affiliation or beliefs of the remaining 20 percent nearly 5 percent are Protestant, 3 percent belong to the Czech Orthodox Church, and the remaining 13 percent belong to a variety of other faiths, including 15,000 Jews. One reason for the decline in faith in the Czech Republic is the 40-year reign of communism.

Religion under the Communists

When the Communists took over Czechoslovakia in 1948, their policy toward religion was similar to that taken in other Eastern European countries behind the Iron Curtain: While the atheistic Communists were strongly antireligious, they did allow Czechs to worship in church and to give religious instruction to schoolchildren on church premises. Priests and ministers were generally allowed to conduct baptisms, weddings, and funerals, and religious materials such as educational instruction and hymnbooks could be published but were subject to the same censorship that existed for all publications.

Believers throughout the country, however, could not become Communist Party members and could not work in government service.

Antireligious propaganda was a part of the curriculum in all Communist-controlled schools.

By the mid- to late 1950s, after Stalin's death, restrictions on religious worship were loosened, and a surprising dialogue began in Eastern Europe between Marxist thinkers and Christian theologians, trying to find common ground on which to express themselves. Czechoslovakia was in the forefront of this dialogue, and in 1967 the only Christian-Marxist congress ever held in Eastern Europe took place at Mariánské-Lázně, Czechoslovakia.

The following year, during the Prague Spring, Alexander Dubček removed nearly all restrictions on religious activities. The Bureau of Religious Affairs, whose main purpose previously had been to thwart religious instruction, now became an agency to further cooperation between the Socialist state and the churches.

While churchgoers tended to be old people who clung to the faith in which they had been raised before the Communists took over, the protest movement of the 1980s, led by Václav Havel and others, prompted more and more young Czechs and Slovaks to search for a faith in something bigger than themselves. Havel described this spiritual renewal in his book-length interview *Disturbing the Peace:*

> . . . The endless, unchanging wasteland of the herd life in a socialist consumer society, its intellectual and spiritual vacuity, its moral sterility, necessarily causes young people to turn their attentions somewhere further and higher; it compels them . . . to look for a more meaningful system of values and standards, to seek, among the diffuse and fragmented world of frenzied consumerism (where goods are hard to come by) for a point that will hold firm. . . .

Yet the religious revival did not catch fire in Czechoslovakia as it did in Poland, where the Catholic Church provided a moral leadership that kept the people's minds and hearts intact. Part of the reason for this was that the church was more suppressed in Czechoslovakia than in Poland, where it historically was stronger and more resistant to persecution. Another reason was the Roman Catholic Church's association with the Austro-Hungarian Empire, which dominated the Czech and Slovak lands in the 20th century. Viewing the church as part of the powerful state that was suppressing them, millions of Czechs and Slovaks left the Catholic Church between the two world wars. Some joined Protestant denominations, but many more became indifferent to organized religion.

Nonetheless, in mid-1980s, one courageous clergyman stepped forward to defy the Communists and unite the faithful. Prague's cardinal František Tomášek (1899–1992) invited Polish pope John Paul II (b. 1920) to Czechoslovakia to help celebrate the 1,100th anniversary of the death of Saint Methodius. Although the government refused permission for the pope's visit, more than 100,000 Czechs and Slovaks flocked to the celebration held at Velehrad. The Pope later visited Czechoslovakia in April 1990 and the Czech Republic in 1995 and 1997. Targeted by the party press for his stand against the government, Cardinal Tomášek wrote with characteristic Czech wit the following response in an open letter: "The church here is not the center of political opposition. All it wishes to do is carry on its pastoral and missionary work. . . . Talking of peace and disarmament would only become relevant and effective when justice and respect for human rights prevail."

Cardinal Tomášek continued to support human rights in his country, and on November 24, 1989, as protest demonstrations in Prague swelled, he conducted a mass celebrating the canonization of Bohemia's patron saint, Agnes Premyslid. The service was broadcast on television and drew tens of thousands of people from all over the country to participate and show their support for religion and their disdain for communism. The very same day General Secretary Karel Urbánek agreed to meet and talk for the first time with representatives of Civic Forum.

The Christian Church Today

While church attendance is up since the fall of communism and more young people seem to be coming back to the faith of their grandparents, many leading Catholics and Protestants are concerned that the church is not taking a stronger stand in social and economic issues that affect the new nation. One of the leading spokesmen for this point of view is Jakub Trojan, dean of the Protestant theological faculty at Charles University in Prague, who has written:

Among the first tasks in the field of theology in my country . . . is overcoming the ghetto mentality that both the churches and theology adopted under the communist regime. . . . Today's Catholic theology and mission basically picks up where it left off—say, 40 years ago—as if nothing significant had happened morally and spiritually in the meantime. Perhaps even more troublesome, it picks up as if important moral and spiritual forces had not changed the face of society *before* communism came to power in our region. Secularization was not invented and set in motion by the communists alone.

Trojan and other church leaders call for the Catholic and Protestant Churches to recommit themselves in the political arena—ensuring that the poor and needy are not left out of a competitive market economy and that environmental issues are addressed in the Czech Republic.

While critics are pressuring the church to become more involved in Czech life, some political leaders are trying to limit religion's influence in their society. One example is an amendment to the civil code recently proposed by the Justice Ministry that would make civil marriages, optional since independence, compulsory, as they were under the Communists.

Protesting against the amendment are both the Roman Catholic clergy in Moravia, the most heavily Catholic region, and the Jewish community in Prague. "It is a pity that in the present day and age some parliamentary deputies are unable to view the Church as an integral part of society and still feel the need to curb its influence on life in the Czech Republic," said Czech Catholic bishop Václav Malý.

The Czech Brethren

Among the oldest Protestant denominations in the Czech Republic is the Czech Brethren, also known as the Unity of Brethren and the Moravian Church. This church was founded by followers of Jan Hus in 1457 in Kunwald, Bohemia. Originally a radical religious group opposed to the abuses of the Catholic Church, the Czech Brethren gradually grew more conservative and attracted a wider range of followers. By the 1520s it had between 150,000 and 200,000 members in 400 congregations in Bohemia

The Jan Hus Church in Prague is a center for the Czech Brethren, founded by the followers of Hus in 1457. (Courtesy Free Library of Philadelphia)

and Moravia. Strongly nationalistic, the Czech Brethren developed in the late 1500s the six-volume Kralitz Bible, the first Bible written in the Czech language. Along with other Protestant churches the Czech

Brethren was persecuted by the Catholics when the Czech lands faced defeat after the Battle of the White Mountain. Ministers continued to hold services secretly, and many members fled to Germany, England, and America. In the United States, they set up their own fully independent "settlement congregations." In 1996, the membership of the Czech Brethren in the Czech Republic was 200,000.

The Jews

During World War II the Jews of Czechoslovakia, like those in so many eastern European countries, were rounded up and exterminated in concentration camps. Of those who survived, many never returned but resettled elsewhere. The Jewish ghetto in Prague is remarkably preserved today, with six synagogues still standing. One of them, Alt-Neu (Old-New), was built in 1270 and is one of the oldest synagogues in Europe. But there are no Jews in the ghetto today, although about 15,000 of them live in other parts of the city. Jewish tourists, descendants of those who

Centuries of a proud people's heritage lie in the crowded Jewish Cemetery in Old Town, Prague. (Courtesy Czech Tourist Authority, New York)

THE LEGEND OF THE GOLEM

Some 300 years before Mary Shelley dreamed up Dr. Victor Franken-stein and his creation in an Italian villa, the Czechs had their own human-made monster—one that is inextricably linked to the Jews of Prague and their long history of persecution. According to the 16th-century legend, Rabbi Jehuda Low ben Bezalel of Prague (1520–1609) brought to life a life-size clay statue by putting a piece of paper in its mouth with the Hebrew word for God written on it. Low called his crea-ture the Golem, Hebrew for a "shapeless mass," and ordered it to pro-tect the Jews of Prague from an evil emperor. The Golem, however, soon turned on the Jews as well and had to be destroyed.

The Golem legend has been retold time and again in literature and film. A German silent movie, *Der Golem* (1914), which set the story in 20th-century Prague, was directed by Henrik Galeen and Paul Wegener, who also played the Golem. The film was so successful that the two men remade it six years later. This second version, which retold the original legend, was photographed by Bohemian-born Karl Freund, who later came to Hollywood and directed such horror classics as *The Mummy,* starring Boris Karloff.

In the climax of the second Golem film, the monster murders a man and sets the Jewish ghetto on fire. The Jews and the city are saved by a little girl who befriends the creature and inadvertently removes the magic word from an amulet around its neck. The Golem instantly turns back into a lifeless statue. The striking style of this classic silent film had a direct influence on the famous 1931 Hollywood film *Frankenstein,* in which Karloff played the Monster.

lived and died here, can be found visiting Prague's old Jewish Cemetery, as observed here by writer Michael Chabon:

The Old Jewish Cemetery was on this gray October afternoon filled with German tourists shuffling politely among the graves, their expressions mild and illegible. They called out one another's names, stooped to run their hands over the Hebrew inscriptions and left behind their unimaginable wishes, scrawled onto scraps of paper. This custom is an odd permutation of the traditional leaving of a stone at a Jewish graveside—unique, in my experience, to the old Prague cemetery, where people use bits of rock, pebbles and even their pocket change to weigh down their written supplications, or cram their messages into the cracks in the weathered old tombs.

Although organized religion has been dealt serious blows in the 20th century in Czechoslovakia, it continues to be important for many Czechs today. In May 1995 Pope John Paul II briefly visited the Czech Republic. Part of his mission was to bring Protestants and Catholics closer together in a country where in the past they have often been in conflict: "I come as a pilgrim of peace and love," he proclaimed. In the city of Olomouc the pope canonized a local priest, Jan Sarkander, who was tortured to death by Protestants in 1620. The canonization, however, was a matter of controversy for some Protestants who considered Sarkander a traitor to Czech nationalism. The flaring up of old religious rivalries may be strangely comforting to religious Czechs, when so many of their compatriots seem indifferent to matters of religion. Yet there is a renewed sense of spirituality that many people have experienced since the triumphant events of 1989–90. Havel, himself a lapsed Catholic, when president, expressed what many Czechs must feel:

> I have certainly not become a practicing Catholic: I don't go to church regularly, I haven't been to confession since childhood, I don't pray, and I don't cross myself when I *am* in Church. . . . [However] there is a great mystery above me which is the focus of all men and the highest moral authority . . . that in my own life I am reaching for something that goes far beyond me and the horizon of the world that I know, that in everything I do I touch eternity in a strange way.

NOTES

p. 54 "'. . . The endless, unchanging wasteland . . .'" Václav Havel, *Disturbing the Peace* (New York: Knopf, 1990), pp. 184–185.

p. 55 "'The church here is not . . .'" Gale Stokes, *The Walls Came Tumbling Down: The Collapse of Communism in Eastern Europe* (New York: Oxford University Press, 1993), p. 152.

p. 56 "'Among the first tasks . . .'" Jakub Trojan, "Theology and Economics in the Postcommunist Era," *Christian Century*, March 16, 1994, p. 278.

p. 56 "'It is a pity . . .'" Daniela Lazarova, Radio Prague. Available on-line. URL: http://www.radio.cz/en/news. Downloaded May 20, 2003.

pp. 59–60 "'The Old Jewish Cemetery . . .'" Michael Chabon, "Prague: Lost Era's Last Survivor," *New York Times*, Travel Section, September 26, 1993, n.p.

p. 60 "'I come as a pilgrim . . .'" *Connecticut Post*, May 21, 1995, n.p.

p. 60 "'I have certainly . . .'" Václav Havel, *Disturbing the Peace*, p. 189.

6

THE ECONOMY

Historically the Czech economy has been one of the most active and robust in Europe. In the 19th century, while other eastern European economies were still based on subsistence agriculture, the Czechs were mining coal and building factories. When Czechoslovakia was formed as a nation in 1918, it was considered one of Europe's leading industrial nations. The ravages of World War II and the subsequent takeover by the Communists changed all that.

The Economy under Communism

When the Communists took industry and farming out of the hands of the individual and gave it to the state, they took away much of the incentive of Czechoslovakia's skilled workers and craftspeople. The Czechs prided themselves on their world-renowned light industries, but the Communists shifted the emphasis to heavy industry—machinery and steel. Production of glassware and other consumer products was severely cut back. The state-run factories turned out shoddy products that Czech workers were ashamed to be associated with. The standard of living under the planned economy of the Soviets declined sharply.

The frustration faced by conscientious workers under the Soviet system is graphically depicted in this anecdote told by former Czech president Václav Havel, recalling the year he worked in a Trutnov brewery in 1974:

. . . My immediate superior was a certain S, a person well versed in the art of making beer. He was proud of his profession and he wanted our brewery to brew good beer. He spent almost all his time at work, continually thinking up improvements. . . . The brewery itself was managed by people who understood their work less and were less fond of it, but who were politically more influential. They were bringing the brewery to ruin and not only did they fail to react to any of S's suggestions, but they actually became increasingly hostile toward him and tried in every way to thwart his efforts to do a good job. Eventually the situation became so bad that S felt compelled to write a lengthy letter to the manager's superior, in which he attempted to analyze the brewery's difficulties. He explained why it was the worst in the district and pointed to those responsible. . . . The manager of the brewery, who was a member of the Communist Party's district committee, had friends in higher places and he saw to it that the situation was resolved in his favor. S's analysis was described as a "defamatory document" and himself was labeled as a "political saboteur." He was thrown out of the brewery and shifted to another one where he was given a job requiring no skill. . . . He could now say anything he wanted, but he could never, as a matter of principle, expect to be heard. He had become the "dissident" of the Eastern Bohemian Brewery.

With the fall of communism the Czech economy sprang back with a vengeance. By 1996 there were more than 2,000 private companies in the Czech Republic with a total value of $20.7 billion; they were responsible for 60 percent of national production. Unemployment in June 1993 was 2.63 percent, one of the lowest in Europe. In 1993 the government reported a small surplus. Trade with Germany and other western countries was rapidly expanding. Of all the nations in transition in eastern Europe, none had experienced the consistent growth and economic benefits of the Czech Republic.

The Czech Strategy—Avoid the Pain

There was a reason for this economic success. In Poland and elsewhere in eastern Europe, new governments plunged forward toward a free-market economy and experienced the pain of change and growth. The Czechs, however, took a somewhat easier road. While many state-run businesses were privatized, the Klaus government cushioned the shock of shifting to a free-market economy by continuing to provide government assistance in the form of subsidies to failing businesses. It held tight control over such expenses as rent for housing and utility bills. The government allowed those state industries that remained to operate despite financial failure in order to prevent job losses.

"The Czech strategy is creating admirable stability, but they haven't paid the whole price for it yet," observed Jan Vanos, president of Plan Econ, an economic consulting firm in the Czech Republic. "The Poles and the Hungarians are further along in the clean-up process. The upheaval in the Czech Republic may not be as bad as in other countries, but the Czechs are still going to have to take some hits."

The "hits" began in the mid-1990s. The formerly state-owned Poldi Kladno steel mill near Prague, for example, had to cut its workforce more than half as more efficient Western production took away much of its business. The government helped many workers find new jobs in Prague and other cities, but many of them were making less money than they had before. "So far the economic reforms have really hurt my standard of living," confessed one 50-year-old plant worker. "But every new beginning is difficult. If not me, then my children and grandchildren will see better times."

An Economy in Crisis

The Czech strategy led the nation into dangerous economic straits in 1997. It began in May with a currency crisis. The central bank tried to lessen the blow by expending $3 billion to keep the currency stable. The government, however, was forced to cut spending by 2.5 percent of the gross domestic product (GDP). An insecure economy was only worsened by the terrible floods that struck the country and much of Europe in the summer of 1997.

The Czech Republic underwent a minor recession in 1998, which grew larger the following year. People who were beginning to climb out of poverty suddenly found themselves without jobs as companies cut back to survive. Businesses failed. Some of the young U.S. entrepreneurs who had flocked to Prague since 1991 to start successful companies left for home as quickly as they had arrived.

The economy continued its downward spiral into the new century under the Social Democratic government.

The European Union

By 2002 the Czech economy had stabilized, although the unemployment rate hit a record high of 10.2 percent in January 2003. While at present the Czech Republic remains better off economically than many of its neighbors, it is still a long way from experiencing western European prosperity. In 2002 its GDP was $8,900 per capita. That is nearly twice the per capita amount of Slovakia, but less than a third of the income of the average German.

The current Czech government is pinning its economic future on membership in the European Union (EU), with its close, mutual trade agreement. In December 2002 the EU announced that the Czech Republic—along with nine other countries, including Poland, Slovakia, and the three Baltic Republics—would be formally admitted to its ranks in May 2004. While the Czechs will benefit greatly from the expanded trade, there are lingering doubts. The Czechs are uneasy that this vast organization, dominated by such economic superpowers as Germany and France, will overshadow their small country. For their part Germany and France, among other EU countries, fear that immigrants from the Czech Republic and other new member nations will stream across their borders in search of jobs and undermine their own increasingly fragile economies. Despite these concerns, the Czech Republic, with its skilled workers and small but thriving industries, should have much to gain from the EU.

Czech Industry—From Armaments to Breweries

Czech industry is highly skilled, and workers have a reputation for turning out top-quality, sophisticated products. Western and northern

BREWING BEER: A CZECH TRADITION

"No one 'manufactures' great beer," says Václav Janouškovec, a fore-man at the Pilsner Urquell brewery. "Brewing is a precision craft."

He should know. His brewery, the oldest in the Czech Republic, has been practicing its craft for more than 150 years. Brewing beer in Bohemia goes as far back as the 10th century. In 1295 the town of Plzeň (Pilsen) was granted a royal charter that gave 260 families the right to brew beer. This eventually led to a bitter dispute in the 16th century between the nobility and the common people, who wanted the right to brew beer, too. The conflict nearly led to civil war.

The brewing at Pilsner Urquell established a new technology in the 1840s that has since become a Bohemian tradition. Barley malt is mixed with grain and pure water that has been brought up from deep wells. The mixture is heated, and the starch in the grain is trans-

(continues)

Pilsner Urquell, the oldest brewery in Plzeň, was founded in 1842. Its then-new technology revolutionized the brewing of beer in Europe.
(Courtesy Pilsner Urquell International)

(continued)

formed into sugar. Carefully selected hops—the dried cones of the flower of a certain plant—are added to the brew to give it the distinctive flavor of pilsner beer. The hops-rich brew is simmered in 16 6,500-gallon copper kettles in the boiling room. Next, yeast is added to start the fermentation process that turns the sugar into alcohol. The fermenting beer is poured into oak casks, where it ages for weeks or even months.

Finally, the finished lager beer is poured into tank trucks that deliver it to pubs and restaurants across the Czech Republic. Bottled pilsner is shipped around the world. When Czechs drink a pint of their golden, bubbly beer, they are keeping alive a tradition that goes back a thousand years.

Bohemia is the center of Czech industry, where everything from tractors to precision microscopes is manufactured. Czech cut glassware has been made in northern Bohemia since the 1600s and is treasured around the world; even older is the tradition of making beer at the fine breweries of Plzeň and other Bohemian cities and towns, a craft that dates back to the Middle Ages (see boxed feature). Plzeň (Pilsen, in German) is so closely associated with the production of beer that pilsner, the lager beer made and bottled in Plzeň, has become the name for any lager beer with a strong hops flavor. Presently the Czech Republic is the sixth-largest producer of beer in the world.

A more recent industry is armaments, centered in the city of Brno. The famous Bren automatic gun used in World War II was invented here and later made in Enfield, England. Tanks and armored cars are also produced in Brno.

The chemical industry is another major area of the Czech economy, and plants are found in Prague, Brno, and other cities. Chemists make plastics, paints, medicines, and other products out of the raw materials of coal and oil.

Heavy industry, developed by the Communists, includes steel plants located in Kladno. The Czechs also manufacture cars, trucks, transportation equipment, and heavy machinery.

Agriculture

The fertile river-fed valleys of north-central Bohemia and central Moravia produce a variety of crops, such as corn, rye, wheat, barley, and sugar beets, from which sugar is extracted. Fruit trees in Moravia and Silesia produce apples, pears, and plums, while strawberries and currants thrive in central Bohemia. Never ones to waste anything, the efficient Czech farmers store the overripe fruit in vats, where they are distilled for brandy and liqueurs. Poppy seeds are shaken by hand from the fried poppy heads and stored in boxes. They are used to decorate breads and cakes.

Natural Resources

Forests cover 35 percent of the land. The largest is the great Bohemian Forest in the south. Lumbering is a major industry, and every tree has its particular uses: Conifers are used to build furniture and houses; beech and oak are the raw material for the many barrels, kegs, and vats used in the Bohemian breweries; softer woods are used to make musical instruments, particularly church organs; pine resin or sap is an important ingredient in glues, varnishes, and some medicines.

Mining was the first major industry in the Czech lands. The rich coal deposits of Bohemia and Silesia were first mined in the mid-19th century. In recent years coal production has dropped. The Czech Republic was the seventh-largest coal producer in the world in the early 1990s; by 2000 it had fallen to 15th place. Other minerals found in Bohemia include copper, gold, zinc, silver, uranium, and iron ore. Silesia has deposits of magnetite.

The American Invasion and Local Entrepreneurs

Once relying mostly on the Soviet bloc for as much as 70 percent of its trade, today the Czech Republic has made tremendous strides in trading with the Western nations. Germany is now its biggest trading partner. In 2001, 35.4 percent of its export business and 32.9 percent of its import business was with Germany. In its strategic location between eastern and western Europe, the Czech Republic may become the main conduit for trade between these two regions.

At the same time many American businesses are opening stores and shops in the Czech Republic, including fast-food giant McDonald's and cosmetic firm Estée Lauder. Established U.S. businesses are not the only ones anxious to make money in the Czech Republic. Since 1991 hundreds of young Americans, many fresh out of college, have flocked to Prague to enjoy the city's beauty and its low cost of living, while starting up a business. Americans in their 20s and 30s own discos, copy centers, pizza restaurants, and the first laundromat in Prague. While some stay on indefinitely, many leave in a year or less and return home.

"Money is going to be made by people who take risks," said Matthew Morgan, an American who runs a public-relations firm in Prague. "The Czechs don't know how to make money. They're not trying. They don't know that capitalism is based on hard work."

A McDonald's restaurant is strangely out of place in this old, historic district of Prague, but it and other American companies are big business in the Czech Republic since the fall of communism. (AP Photo/Rene Volfik)

This condescending attitude and the fact that most of the Americans in Prague keep to themselves and contribute little to Czech society has had a negative effect. Many Czechs have grown tired of their "American cousins" and the materialism they represent. They are also learning how to "make money" and run their own businesses.

One outstanding example of a successful self-made Czech business-person is Ivana Juráňová, who worked as a secretary for a newspaper before communism's fall. On her own, Juráňová decided to start up her own business, selling ad space for clients: "All of a sudden I was in the kitchen with a telephone. My only software was a piece of paper and my brain." In a short time she managed to parlay these assets into a $4.5-million company called Medea S.R.O.

As the Czech Republic's transition to a full market economy continues, there will inevitably be bumps and detours in the road ahead. Yet for the long haul it looks as if it will arrive safely at its destination—economic independence and prosperity. As one steelworker put it simply, "People know how to work in our country."

NOTES

p. 64 "'. . . My immediate superior . . .'" Václav Havel, *Open Letters: Selected Writings 1965–1990* (New York: Knopf, 1991), pp. 173–174.

p. 65 "'The Czech strategy . . .'" *New York Times*, October 17, 1993, p. 3.

p. 65 "'So far the economic reforms . . .'" *New York Times*, October 17, 1993, p. 3.

p. 67 "'No one "manufactures". . .'" Thomas J. Abercrombie, "Czechoslovakia: The Velvet Divorce," *National Geographic*, September 1993, p. 21.

p. 70 "'Money is going to be made . . .'" *New York Times*, October 3, 1992, n.p.

p. 71 "'All of a sudden . . .'" Richard C. Morais, "Hong Kong of Europe," *Forbes*, June 20, 1994, p. 69.

p. 71 "'People know how . . .'" *New York Times*, October 17, 1993, p. 3.

7

CULTURE

The culture of the Czech Republic is a fascinating mixture of age-old tradition and modern experimentation. The Czechs have managed to preserve much of what is precious in their past—folk music, art, dance, and folklore—while exploring new ways of expression in the arts. This restless search for innovation is characteristic of much of the best of Czech culture.

Language

The Czech language is a Western Slavic language, closely related to Polish, Serb, and Slovak. Its 34-letter alphabet is loaded with consonants and has very few vowels. This gives spoken Czech a distinctly unfamiliar sound to foreigners. A favorite pastime among Czech intellectuals is creating sentences that do not contain a single vowel. Diacritics, written accents, are found in many written Czech words, especially proper nouns. Stress is always on the first syllable.

Historically the Czech language has had its ups and downs. It remained largely a spoken language until Charles IV made it the official language of Bohemia's government, law, and literature in the 14th century. In the 15th century, Jan Hus reinforced its importance when he preached in Czech to the people of Prague instead of in German, the dominant language of the church in his day. Hus also reformed and simplified Czech spelling in his written works.

The Czech people express their creativity in all aspects of their lives. Nearly every inch of this country kitchen is covered with vividly designed folk paintings. (Courtesy Free Library of Philadelphia)

With the defeat of the Czechs at the Battle of the White Mountain in 1620, the Hapsburgs of the Austrian Empire suppressed their language ruthlessly, realizing all too well its close connection with Czech nationalism. Jesuit priests, in league with the empire, burned entire libraries of Czech books, many of them priceless. By the middle of the 18th century the Czech language was spoken primarily by peasants in the countryside. All educated people spoke German, the language of their Austrian rulers. Only with the dawn of the national movement in the early 19th century did Czech again become the language of all citizens—a symbol of their spirit and desire for independence. New dictionaries and grammars appeared, and the language received its final codification late in the century in the ground-breaking work of Professor Jan Gebauer (1838–1907) of the Czech University in Prague.

Currently Czech is spoken by about 12 million people—more than 10 million in the Czech Republic and Slovakia and another 1.4 million in the United States.

Literature

The earliest literature of Bohemia consisted of church hymns, religious histories, and poetic romances. All of these were written in Latin. Czech literature and language flourished during the Renaissance period, but the subjection of the Czechs by the Austrians was a terrible blow to the country's literary life. A reawakened nationalism, spearheaded by historian and intellectual František Palacký (1798–1876) in the 19th century, led to a flowering of Romantic patriotic literature. One of the finest of these writers was Karel Hynek Mácha (1810–36), whose epic poem *May*, published the year he died, is considered the finest poem in the Czech language. Mácha's verse was characterized by its melancholy mood and deep love of nature.

As the 19th century progressed, naturalism came to dominate Czech literature, as it did elsewhere in Europe. After the cataclysm of World War I, Czech literature became the finest and most exciting in Europe, due largely to three writers: Franz Kafka (see boxed biography), Karel Čapek (1890–1938), and Jaroslav Hašek (1883–1923). Kafka's tales and novels of modern man's alienation from the world around him were among the most influential works in modern literature. But Čapek had a more immediate impact in his lifetime. In his plays and novels Čapek used science fiction and fantasy to express his moral and political ideas. In *R.U.R.* (1921), his most popular play, Čapek created a race of mechanical men he called "robots," a word he invented from the Czech word *robota*, meaning "hard labor" or "servitude." In his novel *The Absolute at Large* (1922), Čapek predicted the use of atomic energy. Along with his brother and frequent collaborator Josef (1887–1945), Čapek also foresaw the rise of Nazism, but his efforts to warn his fellow Czechs of its threat were to little avail. Three months after his death from inflammation of the lungs, German soldiers marched into Prague and took over the country. The Nazi secret police, the Gestapo, came to Čapek's home to arrest him, unaware that he was already dead. Josef died six years later in a concentration camp shortly before the war ended.

Few novels have satirized war as effectively as *The Good Soldier Schweik* by Hašek. In this four-volume epic tale that remained unfinished at Hašek's death, Schweik, a good-natured dogcatcher, is drafted into the Austrian army during World War I and has numerous outrageous adventures. The novel proved so popular that German playwright Bertolt

FRANZ KAFKA (1883–1924)

A young traveling salesman wakes up one morning to find that he has been transformed into a gigantic insect. A bank assessor is accused of a crime that he has no knowledge of committing; he is tried, eventually convicted, and executed. An official in a penal colony demonstrates an ingenious torture machine to a visitor; when it becomes apparent that the machine will be outlawed by the colony's commandant, the official attaches himself to the machine and dies horribly.

These are three of the plots created by the dark imagination of Franz Kafka, one of the most extraordinary and influential writers of the 20th century. Kafka's life was as drab and unhappy as his novels and tales were bizarre. He was born in Prague into a middle-class Jewish family that spoke German. A troubled, sensitive young man, he studied law and then worked most of his adult life as a state insurance lawyer for the government. He wrote in his spare time and published only a few stories in his lifetime.

Kafka's fiction explores the relationship of the human being to society and God and the human's utter alienation from both. Although he often describes unreal and fantastical events, Kafka's cool, precise prose lends them the clear reality of a dream. The cruelty of life and humanity's frustrated search for meaning and salvation as depicted in his novels *The Trial* (1925) and *The Castle* (1926) foreshadow the rise of Nazi Germany, the concentration camps, and the deadening bureaucracy of communism. Kafka died of tuberculosis at age 41. In his will he named what he considered his best books and wrote that "Should they disap-

Brecht wrote a sequel in 1945, continuing Schweik's adventures into World War II.

After the Communists took over Czechoslovakia in 1948, it became, in the words of German novelist Heinrich Böll, a "cultural cemetery." Censorship and an emphasis on social realism, a literary style that mainly served as propaganda for the Communists, kept writers from expressing their true feelings and thoughts. The works of Kafka and other older Czech writers were banned.

Censorship was loosened in the 1960s, and a new generation of writers emerged who used the dark, surreal humor of their predecessors to express their disillusionment with the communist system. In his plays, Václav Havel used absurd comedy and language to satirize mercilessly the

pear altogether that would please me best. . . . But everything else of mine [including his three novels] . . . without exception is to be burned, and I beg you to do this as soon as possible." Fortunately for world literature, his executor and friend, Max Brod, ignored the will, edited Kafka's novels, and found a publisher for them.

*Franz Kafka's fiction was so anxiety-ridden that it gave a new word to the English language—*Kafkaesque—*which is used to describe anything that is bizarre or nightmarish.* (Courtesy Free Library of Philadelphia)

soulless bureaucracy of the communist system. "Like Eugène Ionesco, he is deeply concerned with language and the possibility of meaningful communication," wrote critic William E. Harkins. ". . . He is specifically concerned with the fate of language threatened by the meaningless slogans of a communist bureaucracy."

With the increasing politicizing of writers and intellectuals in the 1970s and the formation of Charter 77 in 1977, many people employed in the arts became targets of persecution for the government. They lost jobs, had their works banned, and were forced, like Havel, to take demeaning jobs to survive economically.

On a trip to Prague in the early 1980s, American writer Philip Roth was struck with the absurdity of this situation:

. . . The workmen at their beer [in the restaurant] reminded me of Bolotha, a janitor in a museum now that he no longer runs his theater. "This," Bolotha explains, "is the way we arrange things now. The menial work is done by the writers and the teachers and the construction engineers, and the construction is run by the drunks and the crooks. Half a million people have been fired from their jobs. *Everything* is run by the drunks and the crooks. They get along better with the Russians.". . . I look at the filthy floor and see myself sweeping it.

Despite the restrictions on their work under communism, some Czech writers were greeted with great critical acclaim abroad, including the novelists Milan Kundera (b. 1929) and Ivan Klíma (b. 1931) and the poet Jaroslav Seifert (1901–86), who won the Nobel Prize in literature in 1984.

Today, in the postcommunist era, Czech writers are free once again to express themselves, and book publishing is a flourishing business. Some of the most interesting Czech writers working today are women. Daniela Fischerová is a leading playwright and short story writer whose acclaimed collection *Fingers Pointing Somewhere Else* was her first work to be translated into English and published in the United States in 2000. Another excellent short story writer is Eda Kriseova, who also wrote the first authorized biography of her friend Václav Havel.

Music

The folk music of Bohemia has had a profound influence on the great classical Czech composers, whose music is played and revered today. Bedřich Smetana (1824–84) used folk songs and dances in his celebrated comic opera *The Bartered Bride* (1866) and other works. Antonín Dvořák (see boxed biography) continued Smetana's tradition and borrowed brilliantly from Czech and Slovak folk music in his *Slavonic Dances*, the work that first brought him to international attention.

Leoš Janáček (1854–1928) brought Czech music boldly into the 20th century with a series of ground-breaking operas. Although he had written many outstanding orchestral and choral works, it was not until a Prague production of his opera *Jenůfa* in 1916 that Janáček, at age 60, was hailed as a major composer. In his often tragic operas Janáček used human speech as a dramatic element in his music and explored extremely complex psychological states of mind in a way opera had not done before.

One of the most prolific of contemporary Czech composers is Jiri Matys (b. 1927) whose many works include the song cycle *Written by Grief into Silence* (1972); *The Urgency of Time* (1986–87), an orchestral work inspired by a Shakespeare sonnet; and *Chirruping* (1995), a suite for three flutes.

Prague has been a musical capital of Europe going back to the time of Wolfgang Amadeus Mozart (1756–91). That great composer wrote his comic opera *Don Giovanni* as a commission for the city's Theatre of the Estates and conducted the first performance of it there himself in 1787. The Czech National Orchestra continues to perform the works of Mozart and other great composers, and an annual spring music festival in Prague is one of Europe's musical highlights.

Nowadays jazz music competes with folk and classical music in popularity in the Czech Republic. Jazz, although frowned on by the Communists, was one of the few art forms not banned following the crackdown after Prague Spring in 1968. "The communists beat up everybody, but jazz was sacrosanct to them because for some reason—maybe Lenin said so— jazz was considered the music of the proletariat [the working class]," said jazz pianist Martin Kratochvíl in an interview.

Within a decade of its founding in 1971, the Jazz Federation, a section of the Czech Musicians Union, had grown to include a membership of some 20,000 people. It had become the only independent body of its kind in Czechoslovakia. Although the federation was responsible for the popular Prague Jazz Days, it took on an importance far beyond jazz. The word *jazz* itself came to mean not just a certain kind of music but, in the words of the federation, "a symbol of creativity, humanity and tolerance." Writers, artists, and musicians and composers of every style of music were members. The Communist government saw the federation as a threat to its authority and started a systematic campaign of harassment and defamation. It withdrew the permit allowing the organization to hold the Prague Jazz Days, which had grown into an international festival featuring not only jazz but rock and other avant-garde music. In 1984 the government banned the Czech Musicians Union from all activities and three years later arrested seven members of the Jazz Federation, charging them

ANTONÍN DVOŘÁK (1841–1904)

The first Czech composer to gain international recognition, Dvořák's best-known work was composed and written as a tribute to the United States. Dvořák was born in Nelahozeves, a village near Prague, where his father was an innkeeper and butcher. He studied music at the Organ School in Prague and became a viola player in the Czech National Orchestra. His first important composition, the cantata *Hymnus,* was performed publicly in 1873.

Two years later he met German composer Johannes Brahms (1833–97), who would become a close friend and mentor. Through Brahms, Dvořák found a publisher for his first set of *Slavonic Dances* (1878), which brought him instant fame. His other compositions include chamber works for small musical groups, songs, choral works, operas, and nine symphonies.

In 1892 Dvořák, by then a professor of musical composition at the Prague Conservatory, was invited to come to America and be director of the new National Conservatory of Music in New York City. He accepted the offer and spent three years in the United States, during which he wrote his most popular work, the *Symphony from the New World* (1893). The symphony is filled with magnificent melodies and the restless, nervous energy so characteristic of Dvořák's work. Many listeners believed that the composer incorporated African-American spirituals and Native American themes into his music. Dvořák later denied that he had done so, but he also wrote, "I am satisfied that the future

with "authorized banned activities." In a trial that gained great attention in the West, five of the seven were found guilty, but only two served short prison terms. The Soviet policy of glasnost had made the Czech government move more leniently than it might have otherwise.

In the postcommunist Czech Republic, jazz is more popular than ever. Jazz artist Kratochvíl has become a major entrepreneur; his company is involved not only in the record business, but also in video, film, radio, and real estate.

The Czech rock scene is a lively one. One of most popular groups is the Cechomor Music Band, a Czech-Moravian folk rock group, that successfully toured western Europe and the United States in 2002.

music of this country must be founded upon what are called the Negro melodies. . . . These beautiful and varied themes are the product of the soil. . . . They are the folksongs of America, and your composers must turn to them. All the great musicians have borrowed from the songs of the common people."

Homesick, Dvořák returned to his beloved Prague in 1895 and died there from a stroke of apoplexy nine years later.

The best known of Czech composers, Antonin Dvořák, was a deeply religious and humble man. He composed his famous religious choral work, Stabat Mater *(1876), after the tragic death of two of his children.* (Courtesy Free Library of Philadelphia)

Art

As in the cases of literature and music, the first Czech art was religious and included paintings, stained-glass windows, statues, and tapestries going back a thousand years. In later centuries Western art had a strong influence on Czech painting, sculpture, and architecture. Many fine examples of the 17th-century baroque exist today in the nation's elaborate castles and churches.

The literal blandness of social realism deadened Czech art in the 1950s and 1960s, but Czech artists did their part to resist. In 1984 graphic designer Joska Skalník devised a way for artists unrecognized by the government to "exhibit" their work. He invited some 300 Czech and Slovak artists to create works that could be contained within a small, lidless wooden box. Nearly three-quarters of them responded. Skalník hid the boxes in a shed on the outskirts of Prague, where they remained until the collapse of the Communist government five years later.

Since then these remarkable works have been seen in the United States and other countries. The range and expressiveness of these "mini-salon boxes" are extraordinary. One, by artist Jiří Štamfest, shows four tiny dolls running down a flight of stairs against a blank wall. Other artists fought against the repression that they felt the box represented. "I felt I had to change it rather than create something in it," said Margita Titlova. "I made a fire out in the countryside and placed the box on it upside down." The fire, which burned a hole in the back of the box, "is like revolutionary action," she added. In 1993 the Czech government proclaimed the boxed art a national treasure.

One leading Czech artist who was spared the problems of censorship for many years was Stanislav Libeňský (1921–2002), who, with his wife and collaborator Jaroslava Brychtová, worked exclusively in glass.

When the Communists came to power in 1948, they allowed Libeňský and Brychtová to work freely, considering glass design and sculpture a nonpolitical decorative craft. But the couple was unable to ignore their consciences. After the Soviet invasion of 1968, they created their monumental *The River of Life*, in commemoration of the modern Czech struggle for freedom. When they returned from the 1970 World's Fair in Osaka, Japan, where their work was first displayed, they were promptly expelled from the Czech Communist Party and forbidden from traveling abroad together.

One of the most influential glass artists of the 20th century, Libeňský's work lives on in some of Prague's most famous buildings, including the National Theater and the Cathedral of St. Vitus. "Glass allows us to form shapes as we penetrate its mass, determine its center and touch its secrets," he once said.

Theater

The theater has been a vital part of Czech life from the religious plays of the early Catholic Church to the biting satires of Havel and other playwrights during the communist regime. The theater has rarely been an elitist art form, but one that Czechs of all classes have enjoyed. When the National Theater opened in Prague in 1883, the money to build it came from the donations of Czechs from every walk of life.

Despite the popularity of folk plays and realistic dramas of village life in the last century, Czech drama has most often been a theater of ideas. The great Moravian bishop, scholar, and educator Jan Ámos Komenský (1592–1670) usually referred to by his Latinized name, Comenius, was also an accomplished playwright. He used drama to give voice to his thoughts and philosophy on education and other contemporary issues. In the 1920s and 1930s the Čapek brothers expressed their critique of modern technological society through their plays. In the pre– and post–World War II years, the Liberated Theater Company of Prague featured anti-Fascist revues performed by the renowned clown team of (Jiří) Voskovec and (Jan) Werich. The ABC Theater, home of this famous troupe, was where Václav Havel's first satirical plays were produced.

One of the most popular forms of theater in the Czech Republic is puppetry. Puppet theaters are an honored tradition in Bohemia going back to the 17th century. The art of making puppets and marionettes and performing with them was handed down from father to son for generations. Professional puppet theaters abound in Prague and other cities and offer fare ranging from Shakespearean-style plays to fairy tales and contemporary satire. One of the best-known and most intriguing puppet theaters is Prague's Spejbl and Hurvínek Theatre, founded in 1945 by Josef Skupa. Spejbl and Hurvínek are father and son marionettes, whose outrageous adventures are accompanied by projected visual images and colorful musical numbers. Today the Czech theater remains, in the words of Havel, "the spiritual home of its time." One of the most timely theatrical productions is *Nagano, the Birth of a Legend,* an opera commissioned by the Czech National Theater to premiere in April 2004. The story of the Czech hockey team's triumph over the Russian team in the 1998 Winter Olympics in Nagano, Japan, is being billed as "an opera in three periods and one overtime."

Film

For such a small country, the Czech Republic has made an extraordinary contribution to the art of the cinema. The first Czech movies were shot by amateur photographer Jan Krízenecký (1868–1921) in 1898, and the

Celebrated Czech filmmaker Miloš Forman is seen here in London in 1971, three years after he defected to the United States following the Soviet invasion of his country. (AP Photo)

first permanent movie theater opened in Prague in 1907. With the formation of Czechoslovakia in 1918, movie production increased rapidly, and by 1922, 34 feature films were being produced annually.

Despite the censorship of the Communists after World War II, cinema flourished in Czechoslovakia with the establishment of a national film school, FAMU. The first director to achieve international fame was Jiří Trnka (1912–69), whose puppet animation brought to life surreal fantasies, often with a political point. The 1960s brought to the fore a new generation of young, innovative filmmakers, led by Miloš Forman (b. 1932) and Jiří Menzel (b. 1938). Forman's *Loves of a Blonde* (1965) was a winning combination of gentle humor and improvisation. Menzel's *Closely Watched Trains* (1966), which won an Academy Award for Best Foreign Film, was a tragicomedy about a young Czech working in a country railway station in German-occupied Czechoslovakia during World War II. Both films were international hits. Forman defected to the United States soon after the Soviet invasion of 1968. He has had great success with films that are particularly American, such as *One Flew Over the Cuckoo's Nest* (1975), for which he won an Oscar as Best Director, *Hair* (1979), *Ragtime* (1981), and *Man on the Moon* (1999), about the life of comedian Andy Kaufman.

Czech cinema continues to challenge its audiences to think and feel. The long tradition of Czech animation is carried on in the work of Jan

Švankmajer (b. 1934), who uses his strange blend of animation and marionettes and dolls to retell such classic stories as *Alice in Wonderland* and the Faust legend. One *New York Times* critic praised his short films for "evoking Poe or Kafka, [and] bringing the menace of the subconscious to life."

Among the most successful of the newest generation of Czech filmmakers is Jan Svěrák (b. 1965), whose warm comedy *Kolya* (1996), about the relationship between a five-year-old Russian boy and a middle-aged Czech musician on the eve of Communism's fall, won the Academy Award for Best Foreign-Language Film. The movie was written by and starred Svěrák's father, Zdeněk Svěrák (b. 1936), a celebrated screenwriter and former radio journalist. Svěrák's more recent *Dark Blue World* (2001) is the real-life story of a group of courageous Czech pilots who fought on the Allies' side in World War II.

"The main route by which society is inwardly enlarged, enriched and cultivated is that of coming to know itself in ever greater depth, range, and subtlety," wrote playwright and future president Václav Havel in an open letter to general secretary of the Czech Communist Party Gustáv Husák in 1975. "The main instrument of society's self-knowledge is its culture: culture as a specific field of human activity, including the general state of mind—albeit often very indirectly—and at the same time continually subject to its influence."

Through freedom and repression, their culture had been a source of comfort and challenge to the Czechs and to the rest of us as well.

NOTES

p. 76 "'cultural cemetery,'" *New York Times Book Review*, December 10, 1989, p. 43.

pp. 76–77 "'Should they disappear . . .'" John Eastman, *The People's Almanac #2* (New York: Bantam, 1978), p. 1,197.

p. 77 "'. . . Like Eugène Ionesco, . . .'" *The Reader's Encyclopedia of World Drama* (New York: Thomas Crowell, 1969), pp. 165–166.

p. 78 "'. . . The workmen at their beer . . .'" *Prague* (New York: Knopf, 1994), p. 120.

p. 79 "'The communists beat up . . .'" Richard C. Morais, "Pioneer Entrepreneur," *Forbes*, June 20, 1994, p. 78.

p. 79 "'a symbol of creativity . . .'" *Rolling Stone*, April 9, 1987, p. 16.

p. 80 "'authorized banned activities'" *Rolling Stone*, April 9, 1987, p. 16.

pp. 80–81 "'I am satisfied . . .'" Liner notes, recording of Dvořák's *Symphony No. 9 (From the New World)*, performed by the Cleveland Orchestra, CBS's Great Performances series.

p. 82 "'I felt I had to . . .'" *New York Times*, November 28, 1994, p. B1.

p. 82 "'Glass allows us . . .'" *Connecticut Post*, March 3, 2002, p. 5B.

p. 83 "'the spiritual home . . .'" *Prague* (New York: Knopf, 1994), p. 55.

p. 83 "'an opera in three periods . . .'" Slam! Sports website. Available on-line. URL: http://www.canoe.ca/Slam030318/oly-cze-ap.html. Downloaded on August 28, 2003.

p. 85 "'evoking Poe or Kafka . . .'" *New York Times*, October 26, 1994, p. C15.

p. 85 "'The main instrument . . .'" Václav Havel, *Open Letters: Selected Writings, 1965–1990* (New York: Knopf, 1991), p. 63.

8

DAILY LIFE

Even before the fall of communism, life in Czechoslovakia was easier than in most countries in Eastern Europe. The Czechs and Slovaks may have been more politically repressed than, for example, the people of Poland, but economically they were better off. Despite a shortage in housing and consumer goods, Czechoslovakia enjoyed one of the highest standards of living in the region. By the early 1980s nearly one-fifth of Czech families owned cars. Many others owned such luxury items as television sets, telephones, and refrigerators. Presently, after a rough period during which the economy floundered, the Czech Republic is doing better. Life is generally good in this time of political and economic transition, but it is far from perfect.

". . . Czechs regard their future with a mixture of hope, apprehension, and confusion," observed British writer Michael Ivory. "Some are embracing every aspect of Western culture, with unthinking admiration; others see old certainties crumbling and are only too ready to look for scapegoats."

The "embracers" are very evident in Prague, which has awakened after a long slumber under communism. The westernmost of the eastern European countries, the Czech Republic has often in the past identified with the West. Now it is able to fulfill its dream of becoming a kind of America in central Europe.

"The Czechs can't seem to explore fast enough all they missed out on during 40 years of communism," remarked American writer Edmund

White on a visit to Prague in the fall of 1994. "They're digging into their own prewar modernist heritage. They're keeping their bars open 24 hours a day, they're translating books from every language, and they're traveling as much as the disadvantageous exchange rate permits. The frantic desire to catch up accounts for much of the exuberance of this thrilling youthful city."

Yet under all the exuberance, some things remain the same. Not all Western ideas have penetrated everyday Czech life. American feminism, for example, with its emphasis on equal pay for women, greater job opportunities, and an end to sexual harassment, is not important to Czech women in general, and they see it as damaging to relations between the sexes. Yet women, performing the same job as men, earn only half their salary. This seems particularly paltry when the average take-home pay of all Czech workers is only $200 a month.

Much of the glitter and luxury that can be seen in stores in Prague and other cities are not within the reach of the average Czech. Such stores are frequented by the lucky Czechs who have succeeded in private business or the American entrepreneurs who have made a killing in the new consumer market.

A small but vocal minority has sought out scapegoats on whom to pin the blame for their problems. Romanies, Vietnamese immigrants, and other ethnic groups (see Chapter 10) have been blamed for taking away jobs from native Czechs and spreading crime and other social problems. They have become the targets of such hate groups as the skinheads.

The Czech Republic has about 4,000 skinheads, more than any other European country, except Hungary and Germany. As in these other countries, Czech skinheads have evolved a subculture with its own literature, music, and antiforeigner, racist philosophy. Orlík, the leading skinhead band in the Czech Republic, sold 120,000 copies of its first record album. Skinhead magazines, called "skinzines," preach a brand of racial hatred that is disturbingly similar to Nazism and includes material from American hate groups such as the White Aryan Resistance.

The majority of Czechs, however, shun such extremism. They may be unhappy and somewhat disillusioned, but they carry on. As they coexisted with communism, so they will manage to coexist with the transition to a more democratic way of life. "The Czechs aren't as mad as the Poles," journalist Lulos Beniak has pointed out. "They know it's time to pay a price for what happened in the past. People know there is a lot to be done and will tighten their belts."

Perhaps one of the main reasons the Czechs look forward to the future with some confidence is because they are relatively well educated. Indeed, the Czech educational system is one of the finest in Europe.

Education

Education has been a major concern in the Czech lands since the Middle Ages. Moravian bishop Jan Ámos Komenský is generally acknowledged as the father of Czech learning. Among the radical ideas that he promulgated are that teaching should be done in the student's native language and not Latin, that languages are best taught conversationally, and that education should be free, universal, and available to both boys and girls. He also wrote one of the world's first picture books for children, *Orbis sensualium pictus (The Visible World)*, in 1658, in which he emphasized contact with objects in a child's immediate environment as a way to relate learning to everyday life. Komenský's books on how to educate children formed the cornerstone of the Czech educational system.

However, when the Communists took over Czechoslovakia in 1948, they made major changes to the educational system. Independent thought and creativity were discouraged. Memorization and the learning of detailed knowledge were emphasized. All schools had to adhere to one rigid curriculum. Czech students came to excel in math and science, a trend that still holds true, whereas they did far less well in comparative testing in the liberal arts.

Since the downfall of communism, the educational system is slowly changing. The Education Ministry is in the process of phasing out gradually a national curriculum in favor of a more general and flexible one. The government is giving teachers and administrators more freedom in what they teach and how they teach it.

"Teachers now have more chance to approach their work in a more creative way," said Jan Tupý, deputy head of the Education Research Institute in Prague. "The most important change is that although the framework is prepared by the state, the fine-tuning is left up to individual schools and teachers."

At present, all Czech children must go to primary school from the ages of six to 15. The academic curriculum is rigorous. Students in sixth grade, for example, take as many as eight subjects in 45-minute classes. Because most Czech families have two working parents, most elementary students go to *dorgina* (day care) after school until their parents arrive home.

After they have completed their ninth year of schooling, about half of all children enter the workforce, often beginning with a three-year apprentice program. The remaining students continue their education at the secondary level, the equivalent of U.S. high school. Those who choose may go to technical school to learn a trade. At age 19 those students who qualify by examination may attend one of the more than a dozen universities in the Czech Republic.

Sports and Recreation

A fit body is as important to the Czechs as an able mind, so physical exercise begins at an early age. During summer vacation many Czech children attend special holiday-camps in the mountains where they hike, camp, and play team sports, such as soccer, volleyball, and handball. Soccer is the most popular team sport in the country, as it is in many European countries. Tennis is among the most popular individual sports. Under the Communists, there was a national tennis program that trained 30,000 players. Of these, the most renowned are semiretired world champion Martina Navratilova and Ivan Lendl, both of whom now live in the United States. The Skoda Czech Open, a tennis tournament, is held in Prague every August.

The sport with the longest tradition in the Czech Republic is gymnastics. Gymnastics clubs called *sokols* (meaning "falcons" in Czech) were centers of physical activity where trainers instilled young gymnasts with a sense of patriotism as well as self-discipline. The *sokols* were an important part of the Slavic nationalistic movement that began in the mid-19th century. It was this spirit of nationhood that caused the Communists to abolish the *sokols* in 1948, although they continued to train gymnasts, the best of whom went on to compete in the Olympics.

At the 1998 Winter Olympic Games in Nagano, Japan, the Czech hockey team scored a major upset by defeating the Russian team, 1-0, for the gold medal. Czech athletes won eight medals, including two gold medals, at the 2000 Summer Olympic Games in Sydney, Australia. At the 2002 Winter Games in Salt Lake City, Utah, Czech athletes took two medals, including a gold medal for freestyle skiing won by Aleš Valenta in the men's aerials finals.

As important as the Olympics in the Czech Republic is the Spartakiade, an eight-day national exercise competition held once every five years in Prague during the month of June. More than 70,000 participants compete in gymnastics contests, dance performances, and army drills that are watched by millions of Czechs and Slovaks.

Favorite winter sports are skiing and ice hockey, which after soccer is the Czech Republic's most popular sport. The progress of the teams of the Elite League, the Czech equivalent to the United States's National Hockey League (NHL), are followed avidly by sports fans. The hockey team Slavia Praha made international sports headlines in early 1995 when it hired the youngest hockey player in professional hockey history—15-year-old Jan Horáček. Horáček has since gone on to play on several NHL teams and currently plays defense for the Edmonton Oilers in Canada. From 1999 to 2001 the Czechs won three consecutive World Hockey Cups, beating Slovakia in 2000 and Finland in 2001.

Food and Drink

Czech food has benefited, as the country's culture in general has, from geography. Located at the crossroads of Europe, Czech cuisine has taken the best from a number of its neighbors, including the spicy meat stew called goulash from Hungary, schnitzel (veal cutlet) from Austria, soured foods from Russia, and sauerkraut and dumplings from Germany. Roast pork, dumplings, and sauerkraut is the Czech national dish.

Dumplings are a national passion, and the Czechs make them every way imaginable. They stuff them with bacon or cheese and fill dessert dumplings with fruits, such as apricots and plums. Prague hams are among the finest in Europe, and the fish carp is a favorite dish at Christmas. Czech breads and pastries, often covered in poppy seeds, are hearty and delicious. Whatever they eat for dinner, the Czechs like to wash it down with a bottle or two of their native beverage—pilsner beer. Moravian wines are also popular.

FROM CASTLE TO CASTLE

A favorite leisure pastime in the Czech Republic is castle hunting. With thousands of castles scattered across the countryside of Bohemia and Moravia, a devoted castle-lover can keep busy for a long, long time.

One of the most spectacular castles for visitors is Karlštejn Castle, southwest of Prague, which was built by Charles IV between 1348 and 1357. Erected on terraces of a limestone rock, it consists of numerous buildings. The most famous of these is the Big Tower; it contains the Chapel of the Holy Rood, which is the home of the imperial jewels, holy relics of the saints, and the crown of St. Wenceslas, one of the most stunning pieces of Gothic goldsmithing in existence.

Also near Prague is Křivoklát Castle, located in the middle of a forest. The castle dates at least as far back as 1110 but is best known for its late-Gothic additions from the 15th century. Its Great Hall of the

Karlštejn Castle, southwest of Prague, is just one of the thousands of castles that dot the Czech landscape. (Courtesy Czech Tourist Authority, New York)

Royal Palace has a celebrated collection of statues and paintings from this period.

Further south and east of Prague is Český Šternberk, one of Bohemia's best-preserved Gothic castles. Built on a narrow promontory above the Sázava River for defensive purposes, the castle is remarkable for being owned by a single noble family until the middle of the 20th century.

Moravia has castles, too. One of the most famous is Bouzov Castle, which served as the headquarters of the Teutonic Knights for nearly two and a half centuries. Its deep dungeons and torture chambers were admired by Nazi leader Heinrich Himmler, who turned the castle into his private retreat during the German occupation of World War II. Nowadays Bouzov Castle's rich atmosphere is often put to use as a movie set.

Filled with mementos of distant and recent history, the castles of the Czech Republic are true treasure houses of the past.

The Media

The Czechs are big readers who are very interested in what is going on in the world around them. The circulation rate of newspapers in the Czech Republic is 368 per 1,000 people. The press, enjoying its newfound freedom after four decades of communist censorship, is often highly critical of public officials and is often at odds with the government.

There is one public television and radio corporation in the Czech Republic, but the most popular television station is the commercial TV Nova, established in 1994 by Vladimír Zelezny, a high-powered businessman and politician. The government has accused Zelezny and TV Nova of biased reporting and other violations. Zelezny's total buyout of the station from U.S. investor Robert Lauder in 1999 led to criminal charges against him. In May 2003 he was fired as director of the station, which is now under the watchful eyes of a newly appointed government broadcast council.

In 2000 there were 150 television stations in the Czech Republic, and more than 3.4 million television sets. The introduction of cable television in recent years has allowed Czechs the opportunity to view Western programming from Europe and the United States, a country they find particularly fascinating.

In 1995, Radio Free Europe and Radio Liberty, two American broadcasting stations that brought news from the West to communist countries during the cold war, moved their operations from Munich, Germany, to Prague at the invitation of the Czech government. Housed in the former Czechoslovak parliament building, the two stations transmit news and information in 19 languages to the republics of the former Soviet Union and Eastern Europe. There are presently 304 FM radio stations, and 31 AM stations and about 3.16 million radios.

The Czech Republic is one of the most computer-savvy nations in eastern Europe. There were about 2.7 million Internet users in 2001, gaining access through more than 300 Internet Service Providers (ISP). There were also more than 4.3 million mobile cellular telephones in use in 2000.

Holidays

Holidays are often a time when the Czechs can look back fondly on earlier times, when life was less complicated. A good example is Christmas. The season begins with Svatý Mikuláš Day (Saint Nicholas Day) on December 6. The Czechs love Christmas so much that they have set aside two days to celebrate it. December 25 and December 26 are known as First Christmas and Second Christmas, and both are state holidays.

Although Christmas trees are found in most Czech homes, they are a recent tradition. Much older is the custom of cutting cherry-tree branches and putting them in water in the kitchen at the beginning of the Advent season. The flowering cherry blossoms are a favorite Christmas decoration and are also a reminder that spring is only a few months away. The girl who picks the branch watches expectantly to see if the blossoms bloom on Christmas Eve. If they do, tradition says, she will happily marry before the new year is out.

Another Czech Christmas custom is the making of Nativity scenes, called "Bethlehems." These scenes, displayed in homes, are much more elaborate than the manger scenes in other countries and can sometimes include a whole village-full of extra characters. These Bethlehems are often precious works of art, lovingly carved out of wood or formed from bread dough that is then painted.

The Easter season is second only to Christmas in importance. On Palm Sunday, known as Květná Neděle in Czech, the Catholic priests bless and hand out to churchgoers pussy willows instead of the traditional palms. Later that day farmers wave the willows over their fields to ensure a good harvest. In some villages, even today, people place the willow branches on their roofs to protect their homes from fire.

Harvest time, once an important part of life in Bohemia, is actually celebrated twice there. Posvěcení is the church consecration of the harvest, while Obzinsky is a secular celebration. During this joyous time, field-workers make a wreath out of ears of grain and corn and wildflowers, and a doll called a *baba* from the last sheaf of grain to be harvested. These two symbolic objects are placed in a wagon and pulled in a merry procession to the house of the landowner. The workers present the wreath to their employer, who shows gratitude for a good harvest by inviting them to a feast with dancing.

Two patriotic holidays are St. Wenceslas's (Svatý Václav) Day, now officially known as Statehood Day, on September 28, honoring the patron saint of the former Czechoslovakia, and Czechoslovak Liberation Day on May 9, which commemorates the liberation of the nation at the end of World War II by the United States and Soviet armies. Czech Founding Day, October 28, remembers that day in 1918 when the republic of Czechoslovakia was founded. It is a national holiday.

NOTES

p. 87 "'Czechs regard their future . . .'" Michael Ivory, *Essential Czech Republic* (Lincolnwood, Ill.: Passport Books, 1994), p. 106.

pp. 87–88 "'The Czechs can't seem . . .'" Edmund White, "Prague's New Face," *Vogue*, September 1994, p. 352.

pp. 88–89 "'The Czechs aren't as mad . . .'" *New York Times*, March 2, 1995, n.p.

p. 89 "'Teachers now have more . . .'" Paula Horakova, Radio Prague. Available online, URL: http://www.radio.cz/print/en/34369. Downloaded May 22, 2003.

9

CITIES AND TOWNS

The Czech Republic is a small country, and although its population is largely urban, most of its cities are small, too. Prague, the capital, is the only city with a population of more than a million people. No other city has more than 400,000 people. However, many Czech cities and towns have a rich history and cultural importance that belie their size.

Golden Prague

Zlata Praha, or Golden Prague, is a nickname that this grand city on the banks of the Vltava River in central Bohemia has richly earned. Of all the great capitals of eastern Europe, Prague alone survived the catastrophes of the 20th century with its heritage intact. Its narrow, cobbled-stone streets, its age-old cathedrals, its artfully designed bridges—all remain, giving it a sense of history that few European cities can match.

There are other reasons why Prague is called "golden." Some say it is the strange golden glow on its venerated buildings in the late afternoon sunlight. Others believe the nickname refers to the precious medieval paintings and their gold leaf—some of the city's greatest treasures. For still others the gold of Prague is the mystical gold of the alchemists, those ambitious early scientists who tried to transform base metals into gold with a mixture of science and magic from the 13th to the 17th centuries. They were invited to live and work in Prague by King Rudolf II, the monarch (1575–1612) who also encouraged the

Two firefighters wade through waterlogged central Prague in August 2002
during the worst flooding to hit the Czech city in nearly half a century.
(AP Photo/Petra Masova)

more substantial scientific contributions of astronomers Tycho Brahe and Johannes Kepler.

Modern-day Prague (population 1,169,800)* may still be golden, but it is not without its troubles. The disastrous floods of the summer of 2002 brought near devastation to the city. In just six months, however, the city's residents did a remarkable job of cleaning up and repairing the damage. By spring 2003 Prague was largely restored to its former self in time for the heavy tourist season.

Other, human-made forces also threaten to tarnish Prague. Since independence, car ownership has skyrocketed. In 2001 there was one car for every two residents. A six-lane motorway that passes through the city center is continually clogged with traffic. The air pollution from gas emissions is matched by the noise pollution from these vehicles. The adverse effects on health and sleep, particularly for children, has led many families to move out of the city to the suburbs and surrounding towns.

Some of the children left behind are at risk for other reasons. Hundreds of them have fled abusive and broken households and are living in the streets, where they are easy prey for prostitution rings. In April 2001 the Czech police broke up an international pedophile prostitution gang, detaining 87 people.

But for many people, Prague's problems have only made its beauty more poignant. "Prague . . . remains today, a spiritual city," notes writer Patricia Hampl. ". . . It remains powerful, as if the landscape of a dream has been brought to life. It is not simply beautiful . . . the beauty is broken. And this draws the heart out of you to it. It is a city that demands relation."

The first settlements established where Prague now stands go at least as far back as the ninth century. King Wenceslas I of Bohemia established an important German settlement here in 1232, and it eventually became the capital of Bohemia. Under the loving care of Charles IV, Prague became one of Europe's finest cities. For three centuries the emperors of the Holy Roman Empire resided there.

The Thirty Years' War began in Prague when Bohemian Protestants threw representatives of the Catholic emperor of Austria out a window of Hradčany Castle in 1618. It ended for the Czechs two years later with the shattering defeat at White Mountain, just outside the city. Although Prague was under Austrian rule for the next three centuries, it remained

---

* All populations given in this chapter are 2003 estimates.

a cultural capital during the 18th century and the heart of the Czech nationalism movement in the 19th century.

As the capital of the newly formed Czechoslovakia in 1918, Prague was a center of literature and the arts between the world wars, nourishing such writers as Franz Kafka and the poet Rainer Maria Rilke (1875–1926). During World War II the city and its people suffered greatly but were spared the devastation of major bombing.

Now Prague is a tourists' city, attracting up to 12 million visitors a year. The most popular attraction and most dominating structure in Prague is Hradčany Castle, a huge complex on Hradčany (literally, "castle hill"), built during Charles IV's reign. It was the residence of the Bohemian kings and more recently was home to Czechoslovakia's presidents. Next to the castle is the splendid Cathedral of St. Vitus, started in the 10th century and not finished until 1929. It contains the tombs of St. Wenceslas and many other Bohemian kings and emperors. Numerous other churches and palaces dot this area.

The Malá Strana (Lesser Town) is at the foot of the Hradčany and is the best-preserved part of old Prague. Across the Charles Bridge, the loveliest of the city's 13 bridges, is located the Staré Město (Old Town). Here lies the oldest part of Charles University, the Carolinum, and the Gothic Old Town Hall with its famous clock containing the statues of the 12 apostles, which move every hour. A dramatic monument to Jan Hus stands in Old Town Square.

While tourists stick to these well-known sights, there is much more to see in old Prague for the more adventurous visitor. ". . . Beyond these well-traversed areas, Prague has a wealth of cobbled alleyways, hidden squares with romantic statues, churches, galleries and museums," writes American correspondent Jane Perlez. "Often a 100-yard detour down a small lane will yield surprising vistas and glorious, intact architecture."

On the right bank of the river lies New Town, built mostly in the 19th century; here is the business center of Prague. In the heart of New Town is Wenceslas Square, actually a wide boulevard bustling with shoppers and tourists who patronize its hotels, shops, and restaurants. At one end of the square is the National Museum, in front of which stands the impressive statue of Good King Wenceslas. The square was the scene of the dramatic Czech resistance during the Soviet invasion in August 1968 and 21 years later saw the demonstrations that led to the collapse of communism.

Old Town Square, despite its age, remains a vibrant part of Prague with its legions of shoppers, diners, and tourists. (Courtesy Czech Tourist Authority, New York)

The Communists left Prague, Europe's oldest survivor, less joyous. While the joy is returning these days, a certain pathos remains. "Prague has the special sadness of being the last of its kind . . ." writes one author. ". . . [It is] a whimsical, spooky and vainglorious town." And a golden one.

Busy Brno and Beer-Making Plzeň

Located in the southeast, Brno (population 376,400) is the Czech Republic's second-largest city and the capital of Moravia. A major industrial center, Brno is known as "the Manchester of Moravia" because of its many textile and spinning mills. Everything from typewriters to turbines is also manufactured there.

A less-than-robust economy has hurt business at Veletrhy Brno, the fair and exhibition company whose annual trade fair is a long-standing tradition. Nonetheless, the company completed a new exhibition hall in Brno in 2003.

This thriving city has also been the site of the Motorbike Grand Prix each August since 1965. The second Global Wordnet Conference on linguistics was held at Brno's Masaryk University in January 2004.

Brno has a long history, predating perhaps any other town or city in the Czech Republic. The limestone hills to the north of Brno contain caves where artifacts of prehistoric people have been discovered. More recently Brno was the headquarters of Napoléon Bonaparte, who defeated the Russians and Austrians in "the battle of the three emperors" nearby at Austerlitz in 1805. Brno later became one of the Austrian Empire's most productive industrial towns. Some of Brno's finest landmarks are the 13th-century Špilberk Castle, with its infamous torture chambers, and Masaryk University, founded in 1919.

Plzeň (population 165,000), in western Bohemia, is an industrial center, too, lying near a rich deposit of coal fields. The Škoda Works, known during the communist era as the Lenin Works, produces armaments, automobiles, and heavy machinery. But Plzeň is best known for its breweries that produce some of the best beer in the world.

Plzeň was founded in 1290 by King Wenceslas II, who turned it into a major trading town. During the nation's violent religious wars, Plzeň remained a Roman Catholic stronghold. Its splendid example of Renaissance and baroque architecture include the towering cathedral of St. Bartholomew that dominates the city's largest square. During World War II, the Nazis made Plzeň a leading producer of German weapons.

MAGICAL WATERS: THE SPAS OF NORTHERN BOHEMIA

In northwest Bohemia is a group of small towns that for centuries have attracted the sick, the sluggish, the overweight, and the well-to-do of Europe. They have come to this region to bathe in and drink from the medicinal mineral springs.

Perhaps the most famous of these spa resorts is Karlovy Vary (population 53,500) also known by its German name, Karlsbad. The town was officially chartered by King Charles IV in the 14th century. It was Charles who, according to legend, discovered its more than 60 restorative springs. Aristocrats and the famous, from Russia's Peter the Great to German author Johann von Goethe, came to Karlovy Vary to relax and improve their health. The town is also known for its exquisite china and porcelain and an annual international film festival.

(continues)

Karlovy Vary is the best known of the spa resorts of northern Bohemia. Its thermal pools are believed to cure numerous ills. (Courtesy Free Library of Philadelphia)

(continued)

Nearby is Mariánské Lázně (population 14,700), often called Marienbad and referred to as "A pearl in the string of spas." Its curative spring and baths are located on the grounds of a 12th-century abbey. Among the resort's most celebrated visitors were Polish composer Frédéric Chopin and King Edward VII of England. Mariánské Lázne is also the site of a number of international congresses and conferences.

Equally renowned is tiny Jáchymov, whose earthly wealth includes not only its springs but mineral deposits of iron, radium, zinc, and cobalt. Polish scientist Marie Curie (Maria Skłodowska) first discovered radium in its original metal state here. Jáchymov is also the most important pitchblende-mining center of Europe.

Centuries ago Jáchymov was known for its silver mines. A coin, called the Joachimstaler, was first struck there in the 16th century. The name of the coin was shortened to *Taler,* from which the English word *dollar* is derived. Next time you spend a dollar, you might give a thought to the lovely spa region of the Czech Republic.

Industrial Ostrava
and Historic Olomouc

Ostrava (population 317,700) in the northeastern corner of Moravia has not fared as well in recent years as its sister cities in Bohemia. The center of the most heavily industrialized region of the country, Ostrava has been hard hit by the decline in heavy industry and coal mining.

In the spring of 2003 more than 100,000 people in the Ostrava region were unemployed. On May 20 of that year, more than 10,000 trade union members from across the Czech Republic protested against the government in the streets of Ostrava. It was the largest antigovernment demonstration in Moravia since 1989. The protesters and their supporters felt the politicians in Prague were unconcerned about their problems. They protested severe cuts in wages, pensions, and social welfare benefits meant to reduce the deficit. "The government is trying to use an equal approach to all the regions around the country," said Peter Vanek, director of the government office of the Moravia-Silesia region, "not recognizing the fact that the region and its problems simply needs more."

A small town during the Middle Ages, Ostrava was strategically important because of its proximity to the Moravian Gate, the entrance to the lowlands. With the coming of the railroad in the 19th century, the city grew in size and population. Among its most famous institutions is a well-known college of mining and metallurgy.

Olomouc (population 103,000) in north central Moravia was struck by serious flooding in July 1997. The city has a long and colorful past. Once the leading metropolis of Moravia, Wenceslas II of Bohemia beat back the invading Mongols here in 1242. In 1469 Matthias Corvinus, king of Hungary, had himself crowned king of Bohemia in Olomouc. It was also here that Austria and Prussia signed the famous agreement in 1850 that dissolved the German Union and reinstated the German Confederation governed by Austria. Olomouc's infamous fortress, long gone, once imprisoned French statesman and soldier the marquis de Lafayette. Olomouc is equally famous for its historic buildings—the Cathedral of St. Wenceslas and two Gothic churches—and the tasty candy and chocolate that it manufactures.

Towns—Large and Small

South of Prague, not far from the Austrian border, lies České Budějovice (population 98,600) on the Vltava River. An important river port and rail and roadway center, the town is most famous for its breweries, some of the finest in Bohemia. Few Americans realize that Budweiser, the best-selling domestic beer in the United States, is derived from Budvar, a type of beer made in České Budějovice (Budweis, in German) for the past 300 years. When not enjoying the local lager, visitors flock to the town's center with its quaint arcaded square that was built soon after České Budějovice's founding in the 13th century.

Zlín (population 81,500) in central Moravia on the Dřevnice River is known primarily for shoes. In 1913 Tomáš Bata, a peasant shoemaker who had studied Henry Ford's assembly line in the United States, opened a shoe factory here. It eventually grew into a remarkably self-sufficient factory community. After World War II the Communists nationalized the industry and renamed it Svit. The town underwent a name change, too: It was renamed Gottwaldov in honor of Klement Gottwald, the first Communist president of Czechoslovakia. It became Zlín again after the fall of communism, and the shoe factory was turned back over to the sons of Tomáš Bata. Zlín is now one of the largest shoe-manufacturing centers in the world, producing 300,000 pairs a week. "We ship cows in one end, shoes out the other," explains factory spokesman Jaroslav Stokláska. Zlín is also the center of the thriving Czech animated film industry.

In the far west, near the German border, lies tiny Cheb (population 33,400). A center of lignite mining, Cheb also produces machinery, watches, and textiles. As a transportation center, it links the railroad with smaller towns such as Karlovy Vary, one of Europe's most popular health spas (see boxed feature). A small Slavic settlement, Cheb was made part of Bohemia in 1322 by John of Luxembourg. The most memorable historic event that took place in Cheb was the murder of Bohemian general Albrecht Wallenstein, Czech leader in the Thirty Years' War. He was killed by his own generals in 1634 inside a 17th-century castle that still stands.

Historically rich, beautifully evocative, and technologically advanced, the cities and towns of the Czech Republic are dramatic evidence of the country's past, present, and future.

NOTES

p. 99 "'Prague . . . remains today, . . .'" Patricia Hampl, A *Romantic Education* (Boston: Houghton Mifflin, 1981), p. 211.

p. 100 "'. . . Beyond these well-traversed areas, . . .'" Jane Perlez, "What's Doing in Prague," *Sunday New York Times*, Travel Section, August 28, 1994, p. XX10.

pp. 101–102 "'Prague has the special sadness . . .'" Michael Chabon, "Prague: Lost Era's Last Survivor," *Sunday New York Times*, Travel Section, September 26, 1993, n.p.

p. 104 "'The government is trying . . .'" Rob Cameron, Radio Prague. Available online. URL: http://www.radio.cz/en/article/40955. Downloaded June 4, 2003.

p. 106 "'We ship cows . . .'" Thomas J. Abercrombie, "Czechoslovakia: The Velvet Divorce," *National Geographic*, September 1993, p. 20.

10

PRESENT PROBLEMS AND FUTURE SOLUTIONS

In his introduction to the collection of writings entitled *After the Velvet Revolution*, Tim Whipple relates an anecdote told around Prague on the eve of the fall of communism:

> The leaders of the Soviet Union, the United States and Czechoslovakia are each granted one question of God. Mikhail Gorbachev goes first. The Soviet leader wants to know what his country will be like in twenty years' time. "Capitalist," says God, at which Gorbachev collapses in tears. George H. W. Bush gloats and asks the same question about the United States, but God's reply is "Communist," whereupon Bush starts to wail as well. Undaunted Milos Jakes, general secretary of the Communist party, asks what the future holds for Czechoslovakia—and it's God who weeps, with pity.

With the unimaginably rapid collapse of the communist system in November and December 1989, God finally seemed to be cracking a wary smile over Czechoslovakia's future.

The smile that began in 1990 may in 2003 be described as more of a grimace as the Czechs face a myriad of problems—some old and some new.

Class Structure and the Economy

After years of an economic boom, the Czechs are presently experiencing economic problems not very different from those in neighboring countries. Where in 1989 there was one class of people struggling together in Czechoslovakia, today two distinct classes are emerging in the Czech Republic—the few who have struck it rich from capitalism and the majority who are still struggling to make it in a new and unfamiliar world. While the average Czech has a higher standard of living than in any other eastern European country, the Czech worker still brings home the equivalent of only $200 a month. The fancy shops and boutiques opening in Prague and other cities are not for these wage earners.

The cold truth is that the lot of the average wage earner will probably not improve any too soon. Catching up with Western economies could take decades, many economists now predict. Even to reach the standard of living of Spain, one of the poorer countries in western Europe, could take a decade or more. While the majority waits for things to improve,

About 3,000 Czech farmers march in Prague on October 30, 2002, demanding equal conditions after the Czech Republic joins the European Union in 2004. (AP Photo/Michael Dolezal)

CZECHS IN AMERICA

There are about a million Czech-speaking people in the United States, more than in any other country outside the Czech Republic. Many Czechs came to this country after 1848, a year of turmoil and revolution in Europe. They settled mainly in the Midwest, as well as in Canada.

Although there are large Czech populations in New York City, Los Angeles, and Newark, New Jersey, the city known as the "Czech Capital of America" is little Wilber, Nebraska, population 1,624 (1998 estimate), in the southeastern corner of the state. Every August, for one weekend, Wilber hosts the National Czech Festival and comes alive with folk dancing, music, and an enormous amount of eating. Czech dishes such as roast duck, dumplings, and sauerkraut are consumed in great quantities. There is even a contest to see who can eat the most *kolaches,* Czech sweet buns. On the second day of the festival, special awards are presented to those who have promoted Czech and Nebraskan culture.

Another small but thriving Czech community in middle America, Spillville, Iowa, made the great Czech composer Antonín Dvořák a little less homesick during the three years he lived in the United States. Dvořák spent his holidays in Spillville and completed his last symphony, *From the New World,* there.

Czech Americans have made valuable contributions to American life. Some of the most famous of them are actor Walter Slezak, Nobel Prize–winning biochemists Carl and Gerty Cori, and business magnates Joseph Bulova (of wristwatch fame) and Ray Kroc, who turned McDonald's and fast food into an American institution. When asked what was the secret of his success, Kroc invariably replied, "I am of Bohemian extraction, and I have always believed in hard work."

the rich will continue to get richer, something that may create some political turmoil for the Socialist government of Prime Minister Vladimír Špidla.

"We are experiencing cultural shock," said Jiřina Šiklová, a professor of sociology at Charles University. "New relationships among the social strata are just now forming. No one knows who will be poor tomorrow and who rich and the new or revamped code of moral and real values has not yet been universally accepted."

Solutions to these economic problems do exist, and some are being pursued. One is to encourage more Czech entrepreneurs by making capital more accessible to them. Money is so tight that those starting a business are often forced to bribe bank officers just to get a loan. By making money more available, banks and the government can stimulate both new businesses and the economy.

Slovakia

October 28 used to be an important date in Czechoslovakia. It was on that day in 1918 that the new nation was formed and made independent from the Austrian Empire, which had ruled it for three centuries. But in 1993, the national holiday had become something of an embarrassment for both Czechs and Slovaks. How do you celebrate a nation that no longer exists? The split between Czechs and Slovaks was peaceful and amicable, but it left a hole in the soul of both people. Unable to work out their differences, they simply walked away from the problem.

While Czech-Slovak relations were uneasy for several years, they have lately been improving. In June 2003 Slovak president Rudolf Schuster (b. 1934) made his first state visit to the Czech Republic since the election of President Václav Klaus. The two spoke of the goals they shared and discussed strengthening economic and political ties between their countries.

Slovakia hopes to join the Czech Republic in becoming a full member of NATO. It currently holds Partnership for Peace status in NATO along with several other eastern European countries. Said Schuster, ". . . the strategic position for us is Trans-Atlantic cooperation. The US, for us, will be a strong partner in the future too."

One dramatic example of Czech-Slovak cooperation can be seen in the Middle East. A peacekeeping group of Czech and Slovak soldiers has been stationed in Kuwait since 2002. "[The soldiers] themselves say it doesn't matter whether you are Czech or Slovak they just work together," pointed out Czech Radio correspondent Vit Pohanka. "So basically you can have a patrol which is half Czech, half Slovak, or it can be completely Czech or Slovak, they say they are in the same boat."

Crime and Racism

Crime experienced an upsurge in the Czech Republic after the end of rigid Communist rule, and it continues to be a serious problem. Organized crime is involved in drug trafficking, money laundering, and prostitution. Anarchists and other homegrown terrorists have been active, and corruption in business and government is an ongoing problem.

The government has been working to strengthen the police force. It has enforced a strict ethics code and merged the police with the Office of Investigation to raise efficiency in crime fighting. The creation of a witness protection unit will hopefully encourage more people to testify against criminals. In July 2003 the Chamber of Deputies voted on increasing the salaries of police officers, custom officers, and prison employees by a third. This motion, however, was undercut by a government proposal several weeks later to let go of up to 3,500 police officers over the next three years for economic reasons. Meanwhile, robberies and other crimes are on the rise and many are committed by refugees who came to the Czech Republic in search of jobs and a better life and have not found them. "[T]hese people live from hand to mouth here, and this of course can be a motive and reason that leads them to mug and rob people," noted Petra Vitoušová, an activist who helps crime victims. "For example, there have been cases where they follow people in a supermarket to steal entire bags of food."

One area of criminal activity that is particularly disturbing is hate crimes. Most of these acts of violence are carried out against Gypsies, the most ostracized and most visible minority in the country. Originally from India, these wandering people, more properly called Romanies, now live in every corner of the world but most predominantly in eastern Europe. There are 50,000 Romanies in the Czech Republic and another 350,000 in the Slovak Republic. Denied full citizenship in the Czech Republic, a majority of Romanies live in abject poverty, many of them unable to find work. The larcenous behavior of a few have made all Romanies suspect to law-abiding Czechs.

A 65-yard-long wall that separated Romany apartment houses from private Czech homes in Ústí nad Labem is taken down under strong criticism from the government. Prejudice against Romanies is widespread in the Czech Republic. (AP Photo/Libor Zavoral)

In 1996 there were 300 reported cases of violent crimes against Romanies, many carried out by skinheads and other white extremists. Some of the attacks are disturbingly bold. In the summer of 1999, 30 skinheads attacked the Romany population of a Moravian village with bricks, guns, and tear gas. In many of these cases police half-heartedly prosecuted the perpetrators. As Maria Tylejovia, a Romany of Česká Lípa in northern Bohemia, told one American journalist, "The police never hesitate to arrest a Romany, but when we are victims, they do nothing."

This is beginning to change, however. In January 2003 four extremists were sentenced to four or more years in prison for a vicious attack on three Romanies in Ostrava.

Acts of racism against Romanies are not only committed by extremists. In the town of Ústí nad Labem in 1999, residents built a wall six and a half feet (2 m) high between themselves and 37 Romany families living in an apartment block. The town's mayor supported the construction of the wall, and other towns have planned to erect similar walls to separate them from these "undesirables."

Then-president Václav Havel saw the wall and these acts of ethnic hatred as a symbol of the Czech people cutting themselves off not just from the Romanies but from the rest of Europe. "[The wall] seems to be getting higher every day," he remarked, "and soon you will no longer be able to look over it to Europe." The Ústí wall was torn down after only six weeks due to international outrage.

The European Union (EU) has pressured the Czech government to put an end to such acts if it wishes to join the economic trading community and in 2003 hate crimes seemed to be in decline. In the summer of 2000 the government created an advisory body to help integrate Romanies into Czech society. A program to recruit Romany teachers is under way to improve the deplorable education system for Romany children. There is also a movement to recruit unemployed Romanies into the armed forces.

Women's Issues

A larger suppressed minority in the Czech Republic is women. Under communism, Czech women theoretically had equal rights with men, but in reality they had few other than the right to work outside the home. There has been little improvement in women's lot since independence. Women performing the same job as men earn about half the salary of their male counterparts. Women hold few positions in government.

Czech women in general are skeptical of American-style feminism, however. They see a strong feminist agenda as damaging to relations between men and women. As a result sexual harassment and job discrimination are still widespread problems.

Nevertheless, some progress has been made. Since 1992 "mothers' centers," community groups where mothers can work together to improve their lives, have proliferated across the country. Their growth is largely the work of activist Rut Kolínská (see boxed biography).

Health

The Czech health care system was left in shambles after the fall of the Communists and is presently undergoing major reforms. Meanwhile, a decline in heavy industry has drastically reduced air pollution and the diseases it can cause. However, gas emissions from the many cars that now

RUT KOLÍNSKÁ, CZECH MOTHER AND ACTIVIST

After she gave birth to her fifth child in 1991, Rut Kolínská decided Czech mothers like herself needed more support than they were getting at home and in the workplace. She had heard about a mothers' center in Munich, Germany, that provided a community support system for women on maternity leave and a place where they could meet, talk, and share information.

Kolínská opened the first mothers' center in March 1992. Since then, she has overseen the establishment of a network of centers that has blossomed to 150 across the Czech Republic. This kind of activism comes naturally to Kolínská, who had founded Mothers of Prague, an environmental group, several years earlier and continues to lobby for parental leave rights for both women and men.

In 2002 Kolínská was named Woman of Europe for the year in recognition of her work. In announcing the award, Ivana Doležalová called Kolínská "an outstanding woman and very needed in this society."

Kolínská was the second Czech woman to win this prestigious award. Journalist Petra Procházková won the previous year for establishing an orphanage in Grozny, Chechnya, for children whose parents were killed in the Chechnyan war with Russia.

clog the nation's roadways has led to respiratory problems for many urban residents, especially the elderly and the young.

But there is another area in which the government is making some headway to better health—tobacco smoking. Czech pubs and restaurants were traditionally a haven for smokers, but no more. A new law that is scheduled to go into effect in 2004 bans smoking in theaters, movie houses, restaurants, and other public places. Restaurants and pubs must designate a special room for smoking. Furthermore, tobacco products, under the new law, can only be sold in designated shops and other businesses.

The smoking ban is opposed by members of the Communist Party of Bohemia and Moravia and the Civic Democrat Party (ODS). "It goes against natural behavior," protested ODS senator Lucie Talmanová.

"Lawmakers should just respect that Czechs simply smoke a lot." But the good news is that Czechs are smoking less. Smoking is down from 37 percent among adults in 1992 to 31 percent in 2000.

Urban Sprawl

As is the case in other major cities in the 21st century, Prague's population is in decline. Residents, fed up with pollution, crime, and other urban ills, are moving to the suburbs, or more accurately, they are creating new suburbs circling the city. While this movement of people is a boon to developers and offers a new life to many Praguers, it brings a host of new problems associated with urban sprawl. The fields, forests, and other open spaces that once surrounded this great city are quickly disappearing, giving way to housing developments and shopping malls. The new suburbanites must waste fuel and time making long commutes by private car to their jobs in the city, while Prague's public transportation system goes largely unused. New roadways to these communities must be built, in addition to utility, water, and sewer lines, putting a further financial burden on city government. Prague also suffers the drain of lost wealth and talent as middle- and upper-class residents move out.

Solutions to these problems of urban sprawl are complicated, but at least two viable ones have been put forth. The Strategic Plan for Prague was developed by the Municipal Assembly in 2000. It calls for extending public transportation to and from the city for commuters, thereby cutting down the number of cars that clog the roadways. It also recommends the building of district centers in the suburbs as a means to offer new residents services and jobs and places an emphasis on conservation to limit new development.

A more ambitious conservation plan is the creation of a greenbelt around Prague, first proposed by former Prague mayor Jan Kasl. This greenbelt would consist of restored forests and fields linked with existing open space and green areas. The greenbelt could only be used for recreational use, including walking and biking along paths. It would create a clear division between Prague and the new suburbs, preventing further urban sprawl. The greenbelt plan will take 10 years to implement, but preliminary work has already begun.

The Environment

Since 1996 the Czech Republic has taken major steps to clean up air and water pollution in this highly industrialized nation. Nuclear power plants have replaced the coal and oil industries as a source of energy in many regions, greatly reducing the pollution produced by these fossil fuels. Natural gas is another cleaner fuel source that the government is recommending for homeowners.

Nuclear stations, however, may create new problems for the environment. The Temelín nuclear power plant, only 35 miles from the Austrian border, was shut down in early 2002 due to generation problems. Austrian politician Jorg Haider and his supporters have called for the power station to be shut down permanently. According to Haider, repairs at Temelín are deficient, and dangerous radiation continues to leak from the plant. In a sharp dialogue with former Czech prime minister Miloš Zeman, Haider called him "a Communist who has tried his hand at democracy by changing his clothes." The Czechs claim Haider is a political opportunist using the nuclear issue to gain power at home.

Meanwhile, radical environmentalists have not found much support in the Czech Republic. Environmental lobbyist Jan Beránek, chairman of the national branch of the Green Party, feels his organization, only 800 strong, is not in a good position to bring about change. "We had some achievements, but many battles were lost," he reflected, "some of them because there was no solid and reliable partner on the political scene."

The Social Democrats, however, are pursuing environmental issues. CSSD senator Petr Samutry has talked to Green Party members about collaborating on a new environmental initiative called Platon (plane tree).

The Czechs have been great problem solvers in the past. They have been in the forefront of history in changing and improving society through social reform, the arts, technology, and political ideology. The lengthy, difficult transition from communism to democracy may present them with their greatest challenge yet. Of all the countries in transition in eastern Europe, the Czechs may be the people best prepared for this challenge. They have known grief and servitude, but they have also known triumph and success. This particular national spirit, at once restless and rock-steady, is best expressed by former president Václav Havel:

It is no accident that here, in this milieu of unrelenting danger, with the constant need to defend our own identity, the idea that a price must be paid for truth, the idea of truth as a moral value, has such a long tradition. That tradition stretches from . . . Jan Hus, all the way down to modern politicians like Tomás Garrigue Masaryk. . . .

When we think about all this, the shape of our present intellectual and spiritual character starts to appear—the outlines of an existential, social, and cultural potential which is slumbering here and which—if understood and evaluated—can give the spirit, or the idea, of our new state a unique and individual face.

NOTES

p. 107 "'The leaders of the Soviet Union . . .'" Tim D. Whipple, *After the Velvet Revolution* (London: Freedom House, 1991), pp. 66–67.

p. 109 "'We are experiencing cultural shock . . .'" *New York Times*, October 7, 1994, n.p.

p. 109 "'I am of Bohemian extraction . . .'" David Halberstam, *The Fifties* (New York: Villard Books, 1993), p. 167.

p. 110 "'. . . the strategic position . . .'" Jan Velinger and David Vaughan, Radio Prague. Available on-line, URL: http://www.radio.cz/en/article/41502. Downloaded June 5, 2003.

pp. 110–111 "'[The soldiers] themselves say . . .'" Martin Hrobsky, Radio Prague. Available on-line. URL: http://www.radio.cz/en/article/39051. Downloaded June 6, 2003.

p. 111 "'[T]hese people live . . .'" Tracy Burns, Radio Prague. Available on-line, URL: http://www.radio.cz/en/article/41212. Downloaded June 6, 2003.

p. 112 "'The police never hesitate . . .'" Thomas J. Abercrombie, "Czechoslovakia: The Velvet Divorce," *National Geographic*, September 1993, p. 29.

p. 113 "'[The wall] seems to be getting higher . . .'" Achim Heppding, World Socialist Web Site. Available on-line, URL: http://www.wsws.org/1999/nov1999/czec-n24.shtml. Downloaded May 12, 2003.

p. 114 "'an outstanding woman . . .'" Mindy Kay Bricker, *Prague Post*. Available on-line. URL: http://www.praguepost.com/P03/2003/Art/0522/news1.php, Downloaded May 22, 2003.

pp. 114–115 "'It goes against natural behavior . . .'" Mindy Kay Bricker, *Prague Post*. Available on-line. URL: http://www.praguepost.com/P03/2003/Art/0501/news1.php. Downloaded May 5, 2003.

p. 116 "'a Communist who has tried . . .'" *New York Times*, January 19, 2002, p. A5.

p. 116 "'We had some achievements . . .'" Mindy Kay Bricker, *Prague Post*. Available on-line. URL: http://www.praguepost.com/P03/2003/Art/0508/news1.php. Downloaded May 12, 2003.

p. 117 "'It is no accident . . .'" Václav Havel, *Summer Meditation* (New York: Knopf, 1992), pp. 126–127.

CHRONOLOGY

c. 500 B.C.

The Czechs and Slovaks settle on the plains of central Asia and Russia

c. A.D. 500

Avars from the East drive the Slavic tribes into their present-day homeland

620

The Slavs defeat the Avars and build permanent settlements

c. 700

Saints Cyril and Methodius bring Christianity to the Czechs and Slovaks

c. 800

The tribes join together to form the Great Moravian Empire; legendary Queen Libussa founds the first royal dynasty of the kingdom of Bohemia

c. 900

The Magyars break up the empire and conquer the Slovaks

921–928

Bohemian prince Wenceslas unites Bohemia and Moravia under a single crown

929
King Wenceslas is assassinated by his brother Boleslav

1355
Charles IV is crowned Holy Roman Emperor and makes Prague his capital

1415
Religious reformer Jan Hus is burned at the stake for heresy

1415–1436
The Hussite Wars pit anti-Catholic Bohemian nationalists against the Catholic Holy Roman Empire; the conflict ends in an uneasy compromise

1526
Ferdinand I, the Hapsburg ruler, becomes king of Bohemia

1618
A Czech revolt starts the Thirty Years' War

1620
A Czech defeat at the Battle of the White Mountain ends Bohemian freedom; Bohemia becomes a part of the Austrian Empire

1867
The Hapsburgs join with Hungary to form the Austro-Hungarian Empire

1914
World War I begins; many Czechs and Slovaks refuse to fight for the Austrians

1916
Tomáš Masaryk and Edvard Beneš help form the Czechoslovak National Council in Paris

1918
The republic of Czechoslovakia is formed under the Treaty of Versailles; Tomáš Masaryk is named its first president

1935
Edvard Beneš becomes president on Tomáš Masaryk's resignation

1938
Czechoslovakia cedes the Sudetenland to Nazi Germany; Edvard Beneš's government flees to London and sets up a Czech government-in-exile

1939
Czechoslovakia is invaded by Nazi troops and becomes an occupied country

1942
The Czech towns of Lidice and Ležáky are destroyed by the Nazis in retaliation for the assassination of Prague's Nazi governor Reinhard Heydrich

1945
Czechoslovakia is liberated by the Soviet Red Army at the war's end

1946
Edvard Beneš forms a coalition government with the Communists

1948
Jan Masaryk, Czech foreign minister, dies under mysterious circumstances; Edvard Beneš resigns; the Communists take over the government

1953
Purge trials end in the execution of hundreds of Czechs and Slovaks

1957
Hard-liner Antonín Novotný becomes president

1968

January: Antonín Novotný is replaced by Alexander Dubček, who initiates liberal reforms during the Prague Spring

August: A Soviet invasion ends Alexander Dubček's reforms

1969

Alexander Dubček is replaced by Gustáv Husák

1977

Charter 77, a human rights movement, is founded by a group of writers and intellectuals

1979

Dissident leader Václav Havel is arrested and sentenced to four and one-half years in prison

1985

Mikhail Gorbachev becomes the new leader of the Soviet Union and begins far-reaching reforms

1987

Gustáv Husák resigns as party leader and is replaced by Miloš Jakeš

1988

Ten thousand demonstrators march in Prague on the 20th anniversary of the Soviet invasion

1989

November: More than 200,000 people march in Prague, the largest political demonstration since the Prague Spring; the Communist leadership resigns and is replaced by a new administration led by Bohemian Party leader Karel Urbánek

December: Marián Calfa, the last Communist leader of Czechoslovakia, negotiates a transition of power; Václav Havel is unanimously voted the new president by Parliament

1990

February: President Václav Havel visits the United States and addresses a joint session of Congress

1992

June: In new elections, the Movement for a Democratic Slovakia gains power and moves toward separation from the Czechs

July: Václav Klaus, former finance minister, becomes prime minister of the Czech Republic; Vladimír Mečiar becomes prime minister of Slovakia; Václav Havel resigns as president in protest against the splitting of Czechoslovakia

November: The Federal Assembly of Czechoslovakia votes to dissolve the country into two new republics

1993

January: The Czech Republic and the Slovakia Republic are born

February: Václav Havel is elected first president of the Czech Republic

August: Russian president Boris Yeltsin visits Prague and signs a treaty with the new nation

1994

January: U.S. president Bill Clinton visits Prague

1995

May: Polish pope John Paul II visits the Czech Republic and Slovakia for the first time since the fall of communism

1996

June: Václav Klaus's coalition government loses ground to the Social Democratic Party in parliamentary elections

November: Klaus's Civic Democrats win a majority in elections for the newly formed 81-member senate

1997

March: The Czech film *Kolya* wins the Academy Award for best foreign-language film

July: Serious flooding threatens one-third of the country

November: Václav Klaus's government collapses, and he resigns as prime minister

1998

January: An interim government is appointed with Josef Tošovký as prime minister; Václav Havel wins a second term as president

May: The Czech Republic, Poland, and Hungary are invited to join NATO

June: The Social Democrats win national elections and form a new government

July: Miloš Zeman is appointed prime minister

1999

March: The Czech Republic votes in favor of joining NATO

2000

May: The Czech Republic defeats Slovakia for the World Hockey Cup

2001

May: A radioactive water leak is reported at the Temelín nuclear power plant

2002

June: The Social Democrats are voted back into office in national elections

July: Vladimír Špidla is appointed prime minister

August: Prague and other areas experience the worst flooding in the country in more than a century

December: The Czech Republic and nine other nations are invited to join the European Union

2003

March: Václav Klaus is elected president

May: The largest antigovernment demonstration in Moravia since 1989 takes place in Ostrava; Czech entry into European Union in

May 2004 is ratified by a 77 percent favorable vote in a national referendum

June: Slovak president Rudolf Schuster meets with President Klaus to strengthen bonds with the Czech Republic

FURTHER READING

NONFICTION BOOKS

Dubček, Alexander. *Hope Dies: The Autobiography of the Leader of the Prague Spring*. New York: Kodansha International, 1993. The late Czech Communist leader tells about the tumultuous events of his life in this excellent autobiography.

Gwertzman, Bernard, and Kaufman, Michael T., eds. *The Collapse of Communism*. New York: Times Books, 1990. A blow-by-blow chronological account of events in Czechoslovakia and other countries in Eastern Europe during the critical years 1989–90 from the pages of the *New York Times*.

Hampl, Patricia. *A Romantic Education*. Boston: Houghton Mifflin, 1981. This Czech-American writer gives a warm and thoughtful account of her travels in Czechoslovakia.

Havel, Václav. *Disturbing the Peace: A Conversation with Karel Hvezdala*. New York: Knopf, 1990. A book-length interview conducted in 1986 between a Czech journalist and his country's then-leading dissident.

———. *Open Letters: Selected Writings 1965–1990*. New York: Knopf, 1990. Previously uncollected essays and letters spanning 25 years, including Havel's famous "Open Letter" to Communist leader Gustáv Husák, written in 1975.

———. *Summer Meditations*. New York: Knopf, 1992. Havel's first book of essays on politics and morality written after he became president of Czechoslovakia.

Klima, Ivan. *The Spirit of Prague and Other Essays*. New York: Granta Books, 1995. Powerful essays about this famous Czech author's life under the Nazis and the Communists as well as current issues in his country.

Littell, Robert. *The Czech Black Book*. New York: Praeger, 1969. A gripping moment-to-moment account of the Soviet invasion of August 1968, drawn from newspaper and other eyewitness accounts.

Navazelskis, Ina. *Alexander Dubček*. New York: Chelsea House, 1990. An excellent, well-illustrated introduction for young adults to the life and times of one of Czechoslovakia's most important modern leaders.

Sayer, Derek. *The Coasts of Bohemia: A Czech History.* Princeton, N.J.: Princeton University Press, 1998. An engrossing narrative by a Canadian scholar.

Sioras, Efstathia. *Czech Republic.* New York: Marshall Cavendish, 1999. An excellent young adult introduction to Czech culture and history in the Cultures of the World series.

Stokes, Gale. *The Walls Came Tumbling Down: The Collapse of Communism in Eastern Europe.* New York: Oxford University Press, 1993. A detailed but readable account of communism's fall and its aftermath in several countries, including Czechoslovakia.

Whipple, Tim D. *After the Velvet Revolution: Václav Havel and the New Leaders of Czechoslovakia Speak Out.* New York: Freedom House, 1991. A collection of revealing speeches, articles, and interviews with Havel, Václav Klaus, and other political figures in Czechoslovakia before the country split in two.

FICTION AND PLAYS

Buchler, Alexandra, ed. *Allskin and Other Tales by Contemporary Czech Women.* Seattle, Wash.: Women in Translation, 1998. Stories and novel excerpts by the Czech Republic's leading female writers.

Capek, Karel. *Absolute at Large.* Westport, Conn.: Hyperion Press, 1989. A classic of science fiction by one of Czechoslovakia's most imaginative writers.

Cather, Willa. *My Antonia.* Boston: Houghton Mifflin, 1973. The tale of the daughter of Bohemian immigrants coming of age in Nebraska and written by a leading American novelist who was herself a descendant of Bohemian immigrants.

Fischerová, Daniela. *Fingers Pointing Somewhere Else.* North Haven, Ct.: Catbird Press, 2000. A collection of seven stories by a Czech master of the genre.

Hasek, Jaroslav. *The Good Soldier Svejk.* New York: Knopf, 1993. An uproarious satire about war and modern society that follows the misadventures of a Czech dogcatcher drafted into the Austrian army during World War I.

Havel, Václav. *The Garden Party and Other Plays.* New York: Grove Press, 1993. Biting satires of the Communist state by a leading writer of the theater of the absurd and later president of the Czech Republic.

Kafka, Franz. *Metamorphosis and Other Stories.* New York: Penguin, 1971. This volume includes some of the most imaginative and disturbing stories written in the 20th century, including the title story of a man who is transformed into an insect.

WEB SITES

Prague Post. Available on-line. URL: http://www.praguepost.com. A weekly newsmagazine with a useful archive search.

Radio Prague. Available on-line. URL: http://www.radio.cz/en. A daily international news service of Czech Radio with many extra features including a virtual tour of Prague.

INDEX